D1565473

THE STORY

of

KING COTTON

Ewing Galloway, N. Y.

AWAITING THEIR TURN AT THE COTTON GIN

THE STORY
of
KING
COTTON

By
HARRIS DICKSON

NEGRO UNIVERSITIES PRESS
WESTPORT, CONNECTICUT

Originally published in 1937
by Funk & Wagnalls Company, New York

Reprinted in 1970 by
Negro Universities Press
A Division of Greenwood Press, Inc.
Westport, Connecticut

Library of Congress Catalogue Card Number 79-107513

SBN 8371-3760-8

Printed in the United States of America

CONTENTS

ILLUSTRATIONS

FOREWORD

A COTTON bale, wrapped in drab jute bagging and bound with iron bands, is a dull insensate clod, yet tingles with adventure if we can be made to feel the hopes and fears and efforts, the comedies and the tragedies that go into its making.

The Story of King Cotton in America is the saga of white men and black men who created a civilization unique upon this ancient earth, a civilization that rose and battled and fell, then struggled up again to play its part in building this republic.

They who serve the King do not regard him as an agricultural commodity, but as a vital force inextricably woven with their daily destinies.

To see our Monarch as he is, we must look at those who set him up.

Colonel Darius Woodville, whose cronies with reason call him "Cunnel Rye," is one type of cotton planter who lived before and just after our Civil War.

The Colonel's father migrated to Mississippi with his sire and slaves from Virginia, bringing the defects of his virtues and a three-point religious creed. He believes first: that his levee won't break; second: he'll make a bumper crop next year; and third: Democratic candidates will stampede this nation.

Even after Lee's surrender he continued to be an incurable optimist, swatting mosquitoes as he borrowed money to feed free negroes, and starting all over again when the Mississippi River swept away everything he possessed except the mortgage. He's a good loser, in lean years eating corn bread with the same grace that next season he smashes European speed laws.

During a wet season the Cunnel cusses high water; in dry weather he cusses high whisky. To the bitter end of this depression Cunnel Rye will hang on by his eyelashes and draw three cards.

This type of planter has about disappeared and given place to business executives.

While he lived Cunnel Rye usually moved two feet in advance of his shadow, George Washington Johnson, colored. The Colonel has gone, but Wash is still with us, indolent, good-natured and improvident, the same old Wash, unchanged and unchangeable through the ages.

These men made the Romance of Cotton, and faced its grim reality.

ACKNOWLEDGMENTS

I have taken my facts where I found 'em, and acknowledge indebtedness to:—

The Acco Press, published by Anderson, Clayton & Co., Houston, Texas.
Dr. W. E. Ayers, Experiment Station, Stoneville, Mississippi.
Anglo-Egyptian Sudan Government.
Association of Commerce, New Orleans, Louisiana.
U. S. Senator J. H. Bankhead, Jasper, Alabama.
Prof. James E. Boyle, Cornell University.
Mr. David L. Cohn, Greenville, Mississippi.
Mr. Stuart Cuthbertson, Washington, D. C.
Major Perry Cole, Louisiana State University.
Mr. W. L. Clayton, Houston, Texas.
The Country Gentleman, Philadelphia, Pennsylvania.
    Mr. Philip S. Rose, Editor.
Mr. Will Dockery, Cotton Planter, Dockery, Mississippi.
Col. J. E. Edmonds, Economist, New Orleans, Louisiana.
Mr. Lev. Flournoy, Scripps-Howard newspapers.
Dean Henry C. Frey, Louisiana State University.
Mr. Alston H. Garside, New York Cotton Exchange, New York City.
Mr. Oscar Johnston, Lawyer, Planter, Banker, Asst. Secty. of the Treasury, Scott, Mississippi.
Mr. S. M. McAshan, Jr., Houston, Texas.
McGee, Dean & Co., Cotton Planters, Leland, Mississippi.

Mr. J. H. McFadden, Jr., New York Cotton Exchange.
U. S. Senator K. D. McKellar, Memphis, Tennessee.
Mr. Carlton Mobley, Atlanta, Georgia.
Mr. Henry Plauche, Secretary Cotton Exchange, New Orleans, Louisiana.
The Saturday Evening Post, Philadelphia, Pennsylvania. Mr. G. H. Lorimer, Editor.
Mr. Stephen Schillig, Leland, Mississippi.
Mrs. Jean Stovall, Stovall, Mississippi.
Hon. Eugene Talmadge, Ex-Governor of Georgia, Atlanta, Georgia.
Prof. E. V. Wilcox, Chevy Chase, Maryland.
Hon. Norris C. Williamson, President American Cotton Cooperative Association, Lake Providence, Louisiana.

I

THE ANTIQUITY OF PANTS

THE Snake outtalked her until Eve got wise and donned a fig leaf. Next a coon-hide, if her taste ran to stripes. Since that dim morn of feminine awakening, generations of Eves, for change of costume, have pestered Adams to buy expensive furs.

As man grew more sophisticated, the skins of animals went out of style and pants became popular. For trousers à la mode our prehistoric ancestors needed cotton, and there it was, growing just as wild as they grew.

The culture and use of this staple is lost in unfathomable antiquity. Five hundred years before Christ, savage Teutons ran half-naked in the forests of North Germany without a thought of woven fabrics. French workmen on the cathedrals of Chartres and Notre Dame, as late as 1200 A.D. wore sheepskin, wool and leather, but were ignorant of cotton garments that China had known from time immemorial.

Herodotus tells us how the patient hands of Indian women plucked lint from the seed, and carded it. Crude wheels spun their yarn and wove it into cloth on hand looms. India matured a system of spinning, weaving and dyeing that for 2000 years had recorded no improvement. Thirty centuries ago they made a cloth so fine that poets sang its praises as "woven wind," while King Hiram of Tyre wafted his galleys westward with sails of royal purple, strong enough to resist the violence of tempests.

Alexander the Great sheltered his warriors under canvas tents of cotton. So perhaps did Attila, the Scourge of God.

Senators in the forum of Imperial Rome wore cotton togas; and the moslem follower of Saladin fluttered a cotton burnous. Egypt's jibba was of cotton, as were dhootie loin cloths of the Hindoo.

Yucatan natives presented cotton garments to Cortez; Mexico covered its nakedness with the same indigenous fibre. The South Seas knew it, as did Korea and Africa.

What of today? No single product of the soil is more universally used. In whatever corner of the globe he may live, the civilized man when his alarm clock rings at morning, gets up from a bed that's varnished with cotton, crawls out from between two cotton sheets, thrusts his feet into cotton slippers and steps on a cotton mat in the bathroom; softens his beard with cotton oil shaving soap, wipes his razor on cotton paper, peels off his cotton pajamas, vanishes behind cotton curtains for his shower, lathers with a different kind of cotton oil soap, dries with a cotton towel and dresses in cotton underclothes. Even his silk socks have fine cotton for heel and toe. Then he rushes down to breakfast at a table covered by a cotton cloth. The hen that laid his eggs was fed on cottonseed meal. The lard that fried his battercakes is cotton lard. With a cotton napkin he wipes the cotton oil from his mouth, snatches up a handbag that's lined with cotton, opens a pack of cigarettes whose cellophane covering is made from cotton, dashes out to sit on cotton cushions in his automobile whose tires are of cotton. Maybe he collides with a cotton truck, then surgeons stanch his cuts with absorbent cotton and swathe him in cotton bandages.

Cotton, cotton, cotton, it touches every man and woman at every minute of our day—cosmetics, candles, high explosives, motion picture films, airplane wings, armature winding, fertilizers, fountain pens, phonograph records—there seems no end to the multiplicity of its uses through life; then we die on a cotton pillow, our shrouds are of cotton, and the undertaker buries us in cotton-upholstered coffins.

2

In days of shining blades and silver buckles on their shoes, of minuets and sparkling eyes, the Province of South Carolina was a charming community. Her sons were brave, her daughters virtuous, yet the planter's family had to be mighty careful about fire. Through winter nights they sat around their blazing logs and picked inflammable cotton from the seed. The stern old aristocratic father dared not take snuff and sneeze, for that would scatter lint like thistledown all over the room. Hand-ginning was a laborious process, pulling off fibre by fibre, but that was their only method of getting a few handsful of lint.

Gay young cavaliers dashed up on thoroughbreds to court the heiress, but could not jump into automobiles and break speed limits to a night club. Nor even go to a movie. Gallants drew nigh the hearth and got a kick out of watching her dainty fingers pluck cotton from the seed. The evening's work of an entire household might result in half a hatful.

Specie was scarce, so King George III instructed his royal governors to accept cotton in discharge of rent on proprietary lands, cotton at the rate of seven cents a pound. A tedious payment, for the fibre of upland cotton then grown in South Carolina stuck most stubbornly to its seed. The roller gin, then common in India, could not be used, therefore the master with his ladies in the mansion, and black slaves in their quarters, kept busily at work turning out a few pounds before they went to bed.

Longer staple varieties of Peru and the silky fibre that grew on islands off the Carolina coast—still called Sea Island—might easily be processed. But Peruvian cotton did not thrive in northern latitudes, and Sea Island staple was negligible in quantity.

Before the Revolution, little cotton was sent abroad from American colonies, although Lanca-

COTTON PICKING TIME—WHEN SOUTHERN FIELDS ARE AT THE PEAK OF THEIR ACTIVITY

shire mills began to make eager bids for all that could be produced.

Most of the Carolina farmers planted small patches to be spun and woven at home, while frontier housewives at wheels and looms were mixing vegetable fibre with the wool of sheep.

American agriculturists knew that vast areas of southern lands which were then a wilderness, could be converted into cotton fields sufficient to clothe mankind. Cotton would grow luxuriantly; their only trouble was to separate it from the seed, and Yankee ingenuity found the way. By a fortunate accident in 1792, Eli Whitney came out of Yale College with a diploma in his hand and went to hunt a job. He sailed for Savannah, Georgia, hoping to be employed there as schoolmaster. Through another stroke of luck Whitney didn't get the job, else we might never have heard of him, but found himself stranded in a strange country. His predicament would have been awkward except for a friend that he made on the sailing vessel, no less a personage than Mrs. Nathaniel Green, widow of the famous Revolutionary general. Mrs. Green saw young Whitney's plight and extended the hospitality of her mansion at Mulberry Grove.

There the inventor-to-be first saw cotton actually growing, and at night helped the mistress and her household pull off lint.

Slow, slow, slow. Pick and think. Pick and think. English spinners were clamoring for staple at high prices, and Whitney needed money. He believed there must be some quicker process of separation. Believed and set to work. For months he shut himself up with the puzzle, then triumphantly flung open his door and brought out the Whitney Gin, practically unchanged to this day.

It is not pleasant to record how Whitney's jubilation was spoiled. His new-fangled contraption, if it really turned the trick, would be so enormously important that thieves broke into his workshop and stole the model. The priceless gin got away from him, and he never realized full value for his rights. Planters wanted it at once, couldn't wait another minute to get a thing that they'd always dreamed of, and blacksmiths everywhere proceeded to make gins in secret.

It became impossible for Whitney to protect himself, so the grateful state of South Carolina awarded him $50,000 cash for public services. North Carolina added $30,000, and Tennessee contributed another $10,000, so the inventor received $90,000 for his device.

"Device" is too small a word, as Whitney's gin proved itself a miraculous factor in building up the South. It created a new civilization, a new empire based on cotton.

Before that period the trend of agriculture had begun to shift from immense acreages in tobacco as a single crop, George Washington himself being one of the original apostles of diversified farming.

Pioneers beyond the Alleghany Mountains were compelled by necessity to produce everything needed for subsistence of man and beast before they could think of a money crop. Then along came a practical machine that separated seed from the lint so easily as to turn back a tide that flowed toward grain and cattle. Thousands of home seekers migrated to our great Southwest, King Cotton's realm today, and within a few years had almost monopolized the business of supplying humanity with staple.

When our bewigged forefathers in three-cornered hats were framing the Constitution, fields of the world produced only a million bales, of which North America grew about 3000 and exported 250. By 1825, with mechanical ginning, our yield jumped to over half a million bales; and in 1850 passed the two million mark.

3

Our rude forefathers in England were ignorant of textiles for many centuries after oriental women had developed a marvelous art. Britons still wore skins of beasts while Peruvian Incas robed themselves in imperial cotton garments that were woven in convents by nuns who compared with Vestal Virgins. Montezumas of Mexico laid upon their cities an annual tribute of fine cloth, one town alone being required to furnish each year two thousand royally decorated blankets.

Not a spindle whirred in Lancashire until sailors

brought home some cotton from the East to compete with wool, and roused a powerful antagonism.
Mighty nobles who bred sheep on their estates
fought the new fabric exactly as American dairymen
and lard producers fought cottonseed oil when it
was first suggested as food.

British wool interests were strong enough in 1712
to enact prohibitory laws. For wearing a cotton
garment the luckless wight would be fined five
pounds, while the shopkeeper who sold it must pay
twenty pounds. A simple piece of muslin cost thirty
shillings the yard.

Yet cotton won its way. Smugglers continued to
sneak in with calico, and Lancashire began to manufacture cloth in secret, pretty much as moonshiners
make whisky for law-abiding Americans.

Villagers set up clandestine looms, hiding from
officers, and wove laboriously until cottage handicraft
turned to machinery, and John Kay's invention again
set England in an uproar. Neighbors rose in fury
against his mechanical fly shuttle, ganged him and
drove Kay out of England. Other daring spirits
such as Wyatt and Hargrove were also mobbed and
exiled.

The next adventurer to brave popular wrath was
a barber named Arkwright who perfected his con-
trivance that spun fine yarn, and laid cottage looms
upon the shelf. From these devices the prodigious
industry of Lancashire has been built up.

Spinning showed such profits that jealous England

didn't want her colonies to engage in it, as they were so much nearer the fields of raw material. The colonial job was to grow cotton while our mother country got rich on cloth.

Exportation of manufacturing machines was strictly forbidden, yet by stealth somebody brought an Arkwright model to New England for illegal operation.

After our Revolutionary War, when the Whitney gin made sure of a dependable cheap supply, looms began to propagate and spindles bred like flies. Thousands of mill hands set to work and New England commerce boomed. A brisk trade sprang up between Northern mills and Southern growers, a trade that steadily increased until the Civil War.

Four years of struggle—1861-1865—shut off New England's cotton, and mills ran only on what little fibre the Federal armies could capture from Confederate States, with small importations from China.

Peace brought a revival of prosperity to New England, for the South then consumed practically nothing. Soon, however, a current set toward the Carolinas and Georgia where experimental spindles were put in operation. Their climate proved milder and allowed additional working hours every year. This advantage, together with an enormous saving on freight, tempted New England manufacturers to move South.

Pioneer attempts at Colonial spinning had been made in South Carolina, but the enterprise did not

take root, so that up to 1905 the South had only half
as many spindles as were busy in the North.   In the
next thirty years new mills popped up like mush-
rooms, until today the Southern spinner is by far
the biggest consumer for our own fields.   Five and
one half million bales were processed last season
(1935-6) within the cotton belt, near a million more
than were spun in 1934-5.   Largely because of her
own increased consumption the huge "carry over"
of 1931-2 was reduced to workable proportions.

Cotton has become tremendously important not
only to the Southern Belt but throughout this nation.
Our staple enters into such multifarious industries
that we can scarcely guess how many Americans now
gain their livelihood from it.   First the farmers who
plow and pick; ginners who remove the seed and
press it into bales; railroads and steamships that
transport raw material to textile factories, to muni-
tion workers, to manufacturers of automobile tires,
an inconceivable variety of uses.

It is estimated that fourteen million American
toilers depend on cotton for their daily bread, and in
their nightly prayers should thank Eli Whitney,
John Kay, Arkwright, and men of mechanical genius
who pointed the way to such a vast expansion.

II

THE ANTE-BELLUM SOUTH

CAROLINA caught fire from the gin invention that saved so much drudgery, and a most enthusiastic impetus was given to cotton culture in Georgia. Merchants as well as planters of Charleston and Savannah made quick fortunes. The Old Dominion took it up, brown tobacco acres being interspersed with green leaves and snowy lint.

In no part of the world were social distinctions more rigidly defined than in Colonial Virginia. Founders of that colony stepped from the brilliant court of Elizabeth into the forests of a new world. The Lord proprietor transported to his estate a small army of gentlemen and indented servants; afterwards the negro slaves. Each formed a class apart, and almost at once established a quasi-system of aristocracy.

The planter's environment bred certain habits of command, fostered a capacity for directing the effort of others and imposed a sense of responsibility for lives that were in his keeping. Above all else he jealously guarded his rights as an English freeman. When liberty languished in Britain, Virginians stoutly resisted every aggression of royal tyrants. One husband, one wife, one home, one God, this was the planter's creed. Nevertheless, he reserved the right to renounce a monarch who violated the ancient compact between prince and people. No other group numerically as unimportant as those Virginia settlers has given to humanity so many statesmen, soldiers, orators, patriots and philosophers.

Slavery had existed in every colony, naturally gravitating to the South, not as a matter of morals but as a matter of money. The South could make profits out of black labor while the North could not. Southern lands were richer, the climate more favorable, and numbers of negroes could be employed on large estates.

Originally the Virginia and Carolina proprietors were men who, through some favorite at Court, had received lordly grants from the King. Kings were generous with what cost them nothing, and lands being plentiful in this unknown out-of-doors, a few square miles mattered nothing either to the King or to the planter. A plantation might be ten thousand acres or a hundred thousand. Nobody knew, nobody cared. Plenty of land. Plenty.

Their wasteful system of cultivation destroyed the land. The owner did not rotate his crops, so when the fields wore out, he moved his slaves to untouched soil. Instead of replenishing old acres, the planter habitually cleared so much "new ground" each season which returned a sure yield. We now see thousands of farms that are considered worthless after forty years of cultivation, whereas European fields that have grown their crops for centuries are more productive today than they have ever been.

Slavery created a small class of highminded men whose position lifted them above all sordid necessities of life, and afforded the master leisure to think of public affairs. Through migration of sons who carried their traditions with them, those early seaboard planters spread a dominant influence across the continent.

Colonel Damascus Woodville lived in a rambling Virginia house that fronted a public road along which passed the westward tide of travel. The traveler did not pass, but stopped in and took it easy for a week or month. Few were brisk enough to escape the master's watchful eye, and once inside his gate they found it harder yet to leave.

When the weekly stagecoach came rattling past, two negro boys waited for it at the top of the hill, one with a bucket of icewater, the other with a pitcher of sangaree. Added to this was an invitation from their master for all strangers to rest beneath his roof. At mealtime the butler went down to the big gate and blew the dinner horn, a summons to the wide, wide world.

If an innocent wayfarer suggested going to a hotel, the butler answered, " 'Tain't nary hotel, and ef twuz Cunnel wouldn't let nobody go to it. He runs de hotel for dis part of de country."

Why shouldn't Colonel Woodville invite all within hearing to partake of his dinner? He had more than he could eat, and no stranger should be allowed to go hungry or thirsty.

The Colonel felt deeply his obligation to those who honored him by making his house their temporary home. They brought political news, told funny stories and kept him informed as to current events. In return they got a few fried chickens, home-cured hams, corn bread, fruit, melons, cigars, wine—and their host admitted that his toddies were good, for Colonel Woodville mixed them himself.

Sleek horses drew his carriage, fat cows waddled to the milking, shiny mules marched before his plows; plump negroes grinned with dazzling teeth at fatter hens that tempted the frying pan.

When the master returned from a journey, every human being on the plantation swarmed around him before he could shake off the dust. He had brought a present for every one. His pockets bulged with pen knives, band combs, tobacco and gewgaws.

Bad years did not hurt him, and he made the good years an excuse for helping less fortunate neighbors. He wrote freely, for accommodation, on the back of promissory notes that were drawn by mere acquaintances. Rich acres gave value to the autographs. When payday came he sold his Virginia plantation and moved to Mississippi.

In the middle thirties, white families had so multiplied in Virginia, plantations had been so divided and subdivided that property owners found their acres becoming insufficient to support the rapidly

increasing negroes. Soil was poorer and poorer, and
masters confronted the problem of providing work
for multitudes of slaves, so that many planters were
forced to seek new fields and a virgin soil. Far-
sighted ones had already looked ahead to Alabama,
Mississippi and North Louisiana. These conditions
sent a tide of migration flowing from the Old Dominion, through the Carolinas, Georgia, and Alabama. Kentucky sent her stalwart sons to semi-
tropical lands along the Mississippi River.

The Virginian would have preferred to live and
die upon Virginia's sacred soil. It was uprooting
his innermost heart to leave the graves of his fathers,
the hallowed memories of youth. But he must consider his family in the great white mansion as well
as hundreds of black folks in their cabins. Like
patriarchs of Israel they led their sunset caravans,
traveling on foot and in carriages, driving their
horses, their herds and flocks. When evening came
the master rode ahead, selected a site for camp and
had the fires built. Hunters who scouted along the
caravan's flanks came in with game, deer, a bear,
partridges. After a satisfying supper, black folks
got out their banjoes, sang and danced and went to
sleep.

When this family of five hundred white and black
reached the new country, they had left behind them
every personal association, and looked solely to themselves. All for one and one for all they smote the
forest and hewed out a home. Negroes laughed and

sang as the walls of the Big House rose beneath their willing hands, leaving only the ornamentation and finish for artizans of nicer skill. Woods were conquered, swamps subdued; forests gave way to fields, and thick green canebrakes of the springtime whitened with cotton in the fall.

The modest house which later developed into a mansion, was originally of logs with a hall through the middle and two rooms on each side, chinked with mud and whitewashed. A log kitchen, not connected with the main building, stood about twenty feet in the rear. Behind the master's dwelling were the "quarters," a double row of cabins that fronted each other across the plantation road. Forty such cabins indicated that Colonel Damascus Woodville had led out from Virginia about one hundred slaves, men, women and children.

This "Big House" was the plantation nucleus. In course of time their kitchen became a laundry, and a new kitchen was built of home-burned brick, laid by plantation hands. It will still be standing when modern structures have fallen into decay. The smoke house, also built of logs, remained in use, but the log corncrib was soon replaced by a new barn in the pasture lot.

In a capacious library all plantation business was transacted, sufficient to keep the master busily employed. Every room had its open fireplace, for wood was plentiful and country folks love a cheerful blaze.

Southern spirit was a queer medley, the chivalry of the cavalier, the hard-fisted self-reliance of the frontiersman, and the lawless braggadocio of the bad man. Our great Southwest was a new land where laws were feeble and men were strong. Flush times, wildcat speculation and happy-go-lucky negligence attracted every known type of adventurer and outlaw. The crossroads groggery became their lounging place, the gun fight a casual incident of their day, while for more genteel and formal slaughter the Code Duello laid down its reasonable rules. It was a region of lynch law, of mob law, of law in a leather holster, not yet a land for courts, juries, and the orderly administration of justice.

At this early period and until after the Civil War few small white farmers settled in the Yazoo-Mississippi Delta where Colonel Damascus Woodville determined to make his home. While the soil was far more fertile there than on the hills, our Delta had grown up into such a jungle of giant trees, dense canebrakes, sloughs and swamps, that an individual pioneer could not clear it for a field. His own two hands, with those of his sturdy wife, were insufficient for a task that required organized labor. On the contrary, a slave owner with dozens if not hundreds of negroes might set them to felling forests, burning canebrakes and draining low spots until sunlight shone on open acres ready for the plow.

Inquiry is often made, "How big were these plantations? How many slaves?", and the question

might as well be asked, "How big is a piece of coal?"
The landholdings were vague. An original proprietor under grant from a King who was just as
vague, reckoned his possessions as reaching to a certain river, and had no idea where that river chanced
to be. Little of the country had ever been surveyed,
which made no difference, for land seemed limitless
and indefinite as the sky. A planter cultivated what
he needed while negroes bred and multiplied.

It is told of one old master that he was jogging
along a plantation bypath where he met a black boy
and reined his horse to ask, "Who do you belong to?"

"Ise yo' nigger, suh," the boy grinned. "Name,
Zander."

A different sort of pioneer also trekked westward
from the Seaboard, a lone young white man with
his fearless wife, and brought all their belongings,
which consisted of one rifle, one axe and a skillet.
To carve a plantation from Delta tangles was impossible so they chose a less difficult hillside near
some creek bottom which would produce corn. As
full partners the couple hacked down trees, notched
logs, and set up their cabin in which to rear a backwoods family—the breed of Andrew Jackson and
Abraham Lincoln, with the same spirit that carried
our frontiers to the Pacific Ocean.

As population poured into a country newly acquired from Indians, more settlers entered home-
steads from the public domain, with clear titles and
accurate boundaries.

Our small white landowners, tenants and share-croppers, descended from such stock, are not always shrewd in money matters. They need very little and rarely over-exert themselves for non-essentials. More ambitious ones hired out as managers on large plantations, gradually buying lands and becoming big landlords. Energy and thrift grew prosperous, while indolence lived on year after year, just lived.

2

About 1834 Colonel Damascus Woodville had gone broke in Virginia through a too promiscuous endorsement of accommodation notes. One splendid son, afterward known as Colonel Damascus the Second, migrated with his father to Mississippi where Colonel Darius was born. Three Colonels in a row is not uncommon, for by Act of the Confederate Congress any white man who wears socks and owns a cotton acre must be saluted as "Kernel."

Damascus the First located in our famous "Delta" of northwest Mississippi, which contains half the arable area of Egypt where golden Pharaohs reigned. The unparalleled fertility of the Nile Valley made it the granary and then the treasure house of the world. Its story comes down to us in songs of palaces and legends of temples, and records of scientific achievement. The history of our own Delta is for the future. It lies between the Yazoo River and the Mississippi. With Memphis at its northern horn and Vicksburg at the south, the crescent of

Yazoo Hills bends away from the Mississippi River like the rim of a ragged bowl, enclosing sixty-five hundred square miles of black mellow soil; a bowl full of leaf mould, decayed vegetation and the erosion of a continent.

Colonel Damascus the First found a low level country with tortuous bayous, magnificent forests of cypress and oak and jungle vegetation that grew luxuriantly. Little or none of the lands had been cleared, and cultivation must be confined to the highest ridges. By "ridge" it is not meant to suggest a definite backbone or elevation. A ridge in the swamp is imperceptible to the eye, and can only be noticed when the river rises to cover low areas. Then it stands out, still dry, a few feet above the universal water.

"Ruthven Plantation," as Colonel Damascus the First named his property, was partly a ridge beside Lake Ruthven, one of those horseshoe lakes that had once been the main channel of the Mississippi River—a useless coil cast off by the huge yellow serpent as he went writhing down the valley.

To produce cotton in such a country was a magnificent gamble, for there was no such thing as a levee or protection from overflow. He took a long shot for big stakes; if the planter produced a crop, a single season might almost make him rich. Then he'd lose it all next spring when the Mississippi destroyed his growing cotton, drowned his cattle, and swept away his cabins.

At his new home, for a generation Colonel Wood-ville had no neighbors who could be reached by anything that resembled a road. His sole contact with the world was through packets that tied up at his landing and carried his cotton to Vicksburg or New Orleans. Isolation forced him to become an independent prince upon his own domains. The property grew everything it consumed for two reasons: first, the difficulty of hauling heavy supplies, and second, because a master must keep his labor employed all the year around. A cotton crop occupied only twenty-seven per cent of their time, and slaves must not be allowed to idle. They'd get into trouble.

Before the Civil War every negro was a trained man, farmer, blacksmith, carpenter, shoemaker. The master could say to one, "You raise hogs," to another, "Make a vegetable garden," and they obeyed. Their smoke house bulged with hams and sides and sausages, the dairy gave them milk and butter. In earlier years slave women spun their own yarns, wove their cloth, and slave tailors fashioned their home-spun garments.

These conditions, under control of a master, should be remembered when we compare an ante-bellum plantation with the same property after the Civil War that gave freedom to the slave, and shackled his master in financial bondage. King Cotton prospered through the splendid idle forties, even through the fifties of political wrangling when war clouds gathered. Then the Great Tragedy of 1861.

Practically every white male marched to the front, leaving women and children behind in care of their slaves, whose freedom hung upon the conflict. An amazing situation, for this writer does not recall an instance of black uprising or harm done to white women and children. With few exceptions, negroes remained on the plantations and cared for their master's family.

From '61 to '65 the South continued to produce cotton, but it could not be exported because Union warships blockaded our ports. Pass over four years of struggle. Forget it, except as to the effects upon cotton.

III

CIVIL WAR AND RECONSTRUCTION

FOUR years of bloody fighting, and eight years of stealage under Reconstruction, paralysed the cotton industry. Cotton was the only commodity that the Confederacy could sell abroad and purchase munitions. Federal war vessels prevented this exchange by a blockade of Southern ports. A few reckless British sailors ran the blockade and carried cargoes to famished mills in Lancashire, but many of their ships were sunk and the contraband trade proved too hazardous.

Because of her necessity for staple, England came near to recognizing the Confederacy, and relations with the United States were at the breaking point.

If Union soldiers won a battle, they seized cotton for New England spindles, while retreating Confederates just as regularly burned every bale that could not be saved.

When the ragged follower of Lee turned away from Appomattox, he left behind him all that he possessed, his word of honor to fight no more, and set his face toward a problem mightier than the gigantic war.

Footsore and dispirited he trudged back home through a land that was desolated with fire and dotted with graves upon which the grass had not yet grown. No crisp green cotton grew in harried fields where cannon wheels had run the furrows. No mules at noonday rested from their toils, for the mules like the men of the country had perished. There were no fences, no hedgerows, no landmarks of peaceable possession. Monuments of defeat stared at him in stark black chimneys rising from the midst of ruins. He read his fulness of misery in the eyes of black-robed women and the pleading of hungry children who begged unsatisfied at their mother's apron strings.

"War is hell," said General Sherman; but this was hell grown cold; the stimulus of excitement had passed, fires were burned out and left the ashes.

His laws had been uprooted, his labor scattered, his property destroyed. What did he do? Weep and complain? Not he. His grim lips closed upon the past while with resolute hands he knocked at the door of the future, and set himself again to the world-old task of the Anglo-Saxon, organization, supremacy, empire.

The South had no civil government and her affairs were in a state of anarchy. Thousands of negro laborers deserted the fields to follow blue-coat armies, pitiful vagabonds who constituted a heavy burden on federal commissaries. Plantations were ruined. What cotton had not already been destroyed, was now confiscated by the United States. Treasury agents grabbed it wherever found under pretense that it had been sold to, or contracted for, by the Confederacy. After the fall of Vicksburg and before the war ended, flocks of speculators pounced down upon the South, buying stolen cotton for nominal prices and reselling it at fifty cents to seventy-five cents a pound. General Grant declared that fortunes were made by men all of whom he knew to be dishonest. Army officers neglected their commands in order to get rich in this illicit trade, and the stench became so offensive that strict orders were issued against it. Civilian speculators were sent out of the country.

Cotton belonging to persons who had borne arms against the United States, together with their lands and other property, was considered as abandoned, and confiscated. The country swarmed with treasury spies and informers who received from one-fourth to one-half of what cotton they found. The farmer had no chance, and only a small portion of seized cotton actually reached the United States Treasury.

Planters set up clandestine gin houses guarded by the Ku Klux, and a few bales were sneaked off at night. Plantation labor became so utterly demoralized by parades and barbecues in political campaigns that planters seriously considered the importation of Chinese coolies.

Armed mobs of blacks terrorized our rural roads at night until the Ku Klux Klan began to ride. Along the highways and byways moved spectral horsemen clad in white, and many a frightened woman breathed easier when she knew that friends were out there for her protection. The true Klan was composed of the highest type of citizen, conservative men who determined to stop this midnight rambling and marauding. Many of the more obnoxious carpetbaggers who could not be reached in corrupt courts were waited upon and ordered to leave. Some were whipped.

The Klan became an amazing political weapon. According to "Private" John Allen, "Whenever we got ready to have a real old-fashioned election we began a long while beforehand, riding through the country at night, polishing guns and shooting off cannon just to let the niggers know we're fixing to have a fair election."

Wash Johnson, colored, explains his view: "You see, boss, its jest dis-away. Here's one crowd o' white men on dis side oratin' an' swearin' dat de niggers shan't vote. Here's another crowd o' white men on dat side cussin' an' be damnin' dat de niggers shall vote. Den de fack is, boss, dis nigger won't go around no place whar votin' is bein' did."

White men bluffed the blacks and stuffed the ballot boxes, resorting to secret unlawful methods until they drove out the carpetbaggers and erected constitutional governments which were approved by the Supreme Court of the United States.

All the romance of southern elections has now passed away. When that spectacular opéra bouffe called Reconstruction was being played upon our southern stage, there was something doing every minute with diverting specialties between the acts. Never before nor since in the farce comedy of humankind has such a jumble of character artists been assembled beneath a single canvas.

The Fire-eating Kernel, the Humble African,
The Stuffer and the Bluffer, and the
    Big
        Brass
           Band
The Bayonet, the Ballot, the Carpetbagger Man,
The Trigger and the Nigger, and the
    Ku
        Klux
           Klan.

These picturesque accessories of the political ten-twenty-thirty-cent show have put aside their paint and wigs. The bulldozer shucked his long white robe and disappeared; the scalawag made his classic skiddoo. Raw Head and Bloody Bones are packed away in camphor. The curtain has rung down, lights are out, the profits and the losses counted. It's all gone now but not until about 1880 did King Cotton recover from the shock.

IV

CROP AND CREDIT

CIVIL WAR, followed by the far worse calamity of Black and Tan rule, pretty well dethroned King Cotton.

The last carpetbag coattail went flopping out of the land and left enduring evil. Nobody except actual witnesses can realize the tensity of those years from 1866 to 1875 when Northern political clubs sent white women as well as white men to live in plantation cabins with negroes and preach their gospel of hate against the whites. For ten years after Appomattox they kept labor so stirred up that with staple selling at a dollar a pound very little cotton was produced.

Notwithstanding a campaign of malicious propaganda ex-masters and ex-slaves soon got together again in the kindliest spirit. Thousands of freedmen returned to their former cabins and cultivated the same land.

Even under military government and before the carpetbaggers were driven out, Colonel Woodville had already set to work. Conditions were heartbreaking. Newly emancipated blacks swarmed around blue coat army posts, where political schemers led them to believe that every ex-slave would be provided with forty acres and a mule from confiscated property of his old master. Reiterated proclamations by federal military commanders failed to convince them that they must work for a living.

If a negro applied to rent a patch of ground, his contract of tenancy must be approved by an official of the Freedmen's Bureau—a constant source of blackmail and annoyance for planters.

Colonel Woodville came home from the war to find that he had no home. Houses and fences were burned, livestock driven off, his fields grown up in weeds and thickets. Even if he had an abundance of labor on the property there was no food to eat, no clothes to wear. The plantation must be entirely restocked. He had absolutely nothing left except his land.

Before it was time to plant the crop of '66 a few negroes came drifting back, just drifting, trying to find themselves. After Vicksburg fell they had risen up and scattered like a covey of partridges. Some followed the Union Army, big black children, dazed and bewildered, staring at a new freedom which they did not comprehend. More and more of them returned to Ruthven, sheepishly, uncertain of their welcome.

"Here I is, Cunnel," Brewster said. " 'Tain't no place for me to go, 'cept back home."

"All right, Brewster," Cunnel Rye smiled at him. "What do you want to do? You're a free man now."

"Yassuh, free an' hongry."

"Would you like to have your same cabin?"

"Sho would, suh."

There they were, the white man, the black man, and neither of them possessed a dime. Colonel Woodville owned thousands of acres, while Brewster owned his muscle, and they formed a partnership. The landlord gave Brewster a cabin and twenty acres of land with such makeshift animals and implements as he could get.

"Brewster," he said, "we'll manage to feed ourselves some sort o' way, until we can sell our cotton. Then split half and half. You get half and I get half."

Here we have the "share cropper" system which became the almost universal plan of cultivation after the Civil War when no laborer owned a mule, a plow, or was able to stay his stomach while he made a crop.

The landlord's sole asset was his soil, each fecund acre being a potential bale of cotton, and those acres proved a quicker asset than government bonds, because long-starved spinners of Manchester and Massachusetts were clamoring for cotton at a dollar a pound. Thousands of textile workers went unemployed in Lancashire, and bread riots made it compulsory for England to get raw material.

The Southern planter could not produce fibre without mules, a gin, labor and rations to sustain his labor. Such necessities cost money, and British banks, with unlimited capital, agreed to finance the ex-confederate farmer, provided every inch of land should be planted in cotton. Nothing but cotton. Not a shilling would be advanced on ten square miles of corn, or a herd of the finest sheep. Therefore, the formerly independent planter became a mortgaged slave, raising cotton for his creditors, as he has since continued to do.

He produced cotton, nothing but cotton, and bought every human necessity on the credit of his crop. Like the Old Man of the Sea, this crop and credit system for sixty-odd years had ridden the farmer who found himself unable to shake it off.

To restock his plantation and keep alive, he became our nation's most lavish customer; bought shoes from Connecticut, bacon from Cincinnati, flour from Chicago, meat from Kansas City, dairy products from Wisconsin and manufactured articles of all kinds. His saddle horse came from Kentucky, mules from Missouri, cloth from Rhode Island, tobacco from Virginia, plows from Indiana. Only Wash Johnson and Cunnel Rye were raised at home. Compare this with conditions before the war when every plantation was a tight little principality sufficient unto itself.

Not by his own fault was the Credit System so fastened upon the planter that borrowing became a religion. Year after year he renewed his notes, and debts had no terror, for one full crop would put him on Easy Street. The yield of 1868 was excellent, prices high; a few debts were paid, and planters began to hope that after all they might get along pretty well on free labor.

2

No agricultural region on earth has such marvellous powers of recuperation as our Yazoo-Mississippi Delta which developed with amazing rapidity and against all obstacles. Aside from a few properties like "Ruthven," up to a half century ago this had been a country of absentee landlords and six-shooter managers. Desperadoes carried their lives in their hands, and gunshot wounds became the most fatal of swamp diseases. Old timers warned the stranger that a white man couldn't live here unless he kept his hide soaked full of whisky to fight off mosquitoes and malaria. All that has changed. Beginning in 1869, levees were gradually strengthened, morasses drained, artesian water made available, and farmers screened their houses. Railroads now crisscross the land, and concrete highways make plantations accessible. Schools, churches, homes. Within living memory this jungle has been converted into one of the most beautiful and well-populated farming regions on earth.

For a long time after the Civil War Father Mississippi paid no attention to their puny levees, but rose whenever he got ready and overwhelmed them. In 1882, for instance, the lower river broke through in two hundred and eighty-four crevasses and swept away fifty-six miles of embankments. A separate chapter will deal with the question of flood control.

Since boyhood, long before the Delta became livable, Cunnel Rye had waded through overflow after overflow only to come up smiling and so very dry as to justify his nickname. A big-framed, ruddy-faced, generous-hearted man, like every other web-footed denizen of the swamps, he tackled the problem of free labor and pinned his faith to a rosy future.

One morning during the eighties, with the gilt-edged collaterals of faith and future—and the formality of a mortgage—Cunnel Rye strolls nonchalantly into a nice bank where he borrows money to finance his crop. He borrows plenty, for the colonel hates to squeeze copper pennies when golden millions are flowing his way.

It may be remarked that in arranging this loan the banker did exactly what the British spinner did in 1866: asked no questions about how much corn and vegetables or pork the colonel expected to raise. The banker inquires only about cotton, for cotton alone will bring home cash to discharge a debt. Therefore Cunnel Rye must plant a big acreage in cotton.

Having a reasonable balance to draw on, the colonel drives back to Ruthven Plantation, whose cultivation will require forty black tenant families, not one of which could dig up a red cent or a change of socks.

Much as the colonel detests it, he must do some mighty close figuring. From January through August, two hundred and fourteen black mouths will eat up the money he has just borrowed.

For two weeks after his successful raid at the bank, the colonel kept busier than a bird dog, making arrangements with tenants. Most of the old families wanted to stay; others felt the tingle of itching feet, a proclivity to ramble and change their quarters. So Cunnel Rye found himself with seven vacant cabins.

Home-seekers came to him from other plantations; one of them, a loose-hung, gangling mulatto named Jake, showed up and opened his palaver:

"Mornin', Cunnel. I'm seekin' a situation."

"All right. Where'd you work last year? How much cotton did you make? Did you pay out?"

Colonel Rye asked the orthodox questions, while Jake, on his side of their bargaining, betrayed no undue excitement until, "Cunnel," he inquired, "how much furnish does you give out?"

That's the vital point. "Furnish" in Afro-American vocabulary signifies the amount and variety of supplies that his boss will provide on credit.

Every Saturday the plantation commissary issues a standard ration, which cautious planters hold to a minimum, so that they lose as little as possible in bad years. Meat, meal and molasses, that's the formula; but tenants lie awake at nights and study excuses to add a few frills, how to get a bass drum for the plantation band, a full-dress suit, most anything. Jake would buy a second-hand submarine if the boss would let him have one on credit.

At yellow Jake's confab in the colonel's office, landlord and tenant agreed that Jake should get one-half of the prospective lint; that one-quarter of the lint should cover his rent, and one-quarter pay for the use of personal property such as mules, gear, wagons, and so forth. So the planter and Jake go fifty-fifty. Included in his land rent Jake gets a cabin, abundant firewood and pasturage for live-stock. He may also have assigned to him ample ground, free of rent, to cultivate his kitchen garden. But Jake rarely bothers about a garden.

Long-staple cotton is the only major crop in the United States that is grown by pauper labor. No matter how much money a negro tenant makes, he always has been and probably will always be a pauper. Let no reader regard this as a wholesale denunciation of our black friends. The high-class planter never blames Jake for his invincible limitations. He may cuss him out with half a smile, but well the colonel realizes that if negroes were thrifty and economical, there would be no place in our delta for any white planter, no function for him to perform. Blacks would own the country. They spend more than enough cash for gingersnaps and sardines to buy the land over and over again. In prosperous seasons, like a baby with a basket of gold, these wastrel children chuck their dollars at the jaybirds without fear of a tomorrow.

Jim Fields was one of the kind who never thought about tomorrow, and was always getting behind with his crop, so Mr. Gordon, Colonel Rye's manager, was always getting behind Jim. During the past three weeks Gordon had kept Jim and family on the jump until they caught up; then as a special favor allowed them to pick in the plantation patch for real money.

The first cash he'd seen that season gave Jim a swimming in the head as he trudged home whistling through the cotton patch toward his cabin.

Three children and a litter of mongrel pups were tumbling together in dust at the door. The biggest child, Jinny, was twelve years old and she wore a garment; the others had not yet eaten of the apple, and didn't even show a fig leaf.

"Jinny," their father asked, "whar's yo' ma?"

"Dar she," pointing to a flat-nosed woman in a blue gingham dress, who came towards them with a bucket of water on her head.

"Hurry up, M'ria, give dese chillun dey supper, den' put 'em to bed. Less all go to de sto'."

Jim had a masterful way about him when he had money, and Maria long ago learned her lesson of obedience. Without a word she caught up the smaller children, dusted them off with her sunbon-

Resettlement Administration Photograph by Rothstein

THE SHARE CROPPER IS A SOUTHERN INSTITUTION

net and half dragged them into the house. Jinny edged up close to her father, the white, upturned eyes shining against the little black face.

"Pa, oh, pa, lemme go to de sto'. I picked a heap o' cotton."

"You can't go in dat dress; wash yo' face."

Jinny skinned off her single garment, pulled on a blue gingham like her mother's, dipped one hand in the tin basin, smeared it across her face—and was ready.

Jim, after more elaborate preliminaries, took his brilliantly striped vest from its peg, and swapped his straw hat for a rakish-looking cap with patent-leather brim. Then he sat on the bed and watched Maria pour the last drop of molasses into a tin platter and divide a piece of hoe-cake equally between the two children. Like starved animals they sopped up every drop of molasses and ate every crumb of bread.

Maria got out her coal-oil can, the molasses jug and the meal sack, all empty.

"Better bring dat biggest basket," Jim suggested. "We'se goin' to have flour, an' sardines, and simon-fish, an'—"

Jinny's eyes bulged as her splendid father enumerated every known delicacy, then stalked out of the door, leaving Maria to follow with Jinny tagging at her heels.

Jim strode along the tortuous path between cotton

stalks, until he struck the "Big Road," at the forks of which stood "The Sto'."

Along the edge of the store gallery sat a row of cotton pickers, men and women, black and yellow. Patient mules waited at the hitching-rack, well knowing that a day of rest followed all this tumult.

The store was crowded. Every chair, every barrel and every box had its listening occupant, listening to the phonograph. Maria and Jinny forgot everything except the music, and wedged themselves in as close as they could get. Jim listened for a moment, then elbowed his way back to the desk at the rear and took his place in the line of cotton pickers who were waiting for their weekly settlement. Presently, it came his turn and he stepped to the window. Mr. Gordon looked up. "Jim Fields." He glanced at his book and rapidly read the items: "Jim Fields, $7.05; Maria Fields, $3.35; Jinny Fields, 90 cents. Is that right, Jim?"

"I reckon dat's all right, boss," said Jim, handing in his tickets. Mr. Gordon passed him out a crisp ten-dollar bill which had never been folded. Jim became its owner—for a few brief minutes. Then followed a dollar, a quarter, and a nickel.

Jim held his money in his hand as he swaggered toward the counter. With five hungry mouths to feed, he knew precisely how little it took to keep them alive. Jim could run over the plantation allowance, backward or forward:

16 pounds dry salt meat	$2.00
4 pecks of meal	1.20
4 pints of molasses	.50
Coffee	.50
Flour	.50
Candles	.10
Matches	.05
	$4.85

Sometimes Jim's family managed to skimp through a week on meat and meal and molasses, $3.70. But that was when times were hard; tonight he had cold cash in his pocket, and there was no need for economy.

Maria had come up beside him and tried to peep into his hand. "How much it come to, Jim?"

"Ten dollars an' a nickel; you didn't do hardly a bit o' work," he snapped back.

Little black Jinny clutched her mother's dress as they lined up at the counter where Blinky Wilson, the pale little clerk with watery eyes, was selling a woman some calico. "Lawdy, Mr. Wilson," the woman objected; "dat's mighty norrer, ain't it?"

"Yes, it is narrow, of course, but just look how *long* it is." Blinky rolled out a bewildering length of gorgeously figured cloth.

"Ten yards—fifty cents!" The clerk wrapped it up, swept the coin into the drawer, and tossed the woman a cake, then turned to Jim with an affable air, "Now, what can I do for you?"

"Gimme a seegyar," he said, and laid down his nickel. "One o' dem long fellers wid a gol' ban' on it." Jim tilted the cigar upward in his mouth and touched it off. It blazed magnificently and crackled. Then Jim strolled up and down the store with hands in his pockets and began to look into the showcases, picking out things he wanted. "Lemme see some o' yo' watches, Mr. Wilson."

"Watches!" It caught the ear of every negro in the store. Two yellow women with a preacher between them forgot their argument and pushed forward. Maria was too proud to suggest economy before this congregation, and glanced at the watch that Blinky passed across to Jim.

"I wants a stem-winder."

"This is a stem-winder; warranted solid German silver—*German,* not common silver."

Jim looked dubiously to his wife. "You see, M'ria," he argued, "we'se bound to have a watch; we don't never know when time comes to quit work without a watch."

Maria said nothing, and, taking silence for consent, Jim turned to the clerk. "Mr. Wilson, what's de least cash money you kin take for dis watch?"

"Five dollars," Blinky answered him aloud, then leaned over and whispered: "but, being as you trades with us regular, you can take it along for three. You make two dollars clear, right off. I'll bet you never made two dollars that easy in your whole life."

"It sho' is easier'n pickin' three hundred pounds o' cotton," Jim assented.

Blinky reached into the showcase, selected a heavy chain with its crystal charm bigger than a hickory nut, and snapped it on the watch. Then he draped an elaborate festoon across Jim's striped vest.

"Now, go back and look at yourself in the glass!"

Jim and Maria and Jinny, the woman with the cake, the preacher and a long line of darkies followed to the mirror.

"Now, Jim," the clerk suggested laughingly, "tell these ladies what time it is by your watch and chain."

Jim fished out his watch and compared it with the clock. "Hit's adzackly fo'teen minutes to six."

"That's a fine watch, Jim, it runs neck and neck with our clock right now, without half trying; it will do a heap better than that after a reliable man like you wears it for a while and teaches it how to run."

Jim dangled the charm before the mirror and considered. "How much you say dat watch is wuth?"

Blinky led him aside. "It's really worth five dollars, net, all discounts off; but you can have it for three. That watch is too fine for our trade; these ignorant niggers around here don't know nothing about a real, good watch."

"Speck I'll have to take it, Mr. Wilson. I can't 'tend to my business no longer 'thout a watch."

Jim studied his ten-dollar bill, then slowly pushed it across the counter.

"Please, suh, gimme change for dat."

"Now, Jim!"—Maria tugged at his coat-sleeve; she could scarcely wait until her turn came—"Now, Jim, I wants dat ban'com', an' a bottle o' dat medicine what takes kinks outen yo' hair—like dat." His wife pointed to the seductive picture of a negro woman who was combing out a silken suit of hair. "You promised it last week, Jim, an' you'se done bought yo'self a watch, an'—"

Blinky stood ready with the celluloid bandcomb and a bottle of anti-kink with that silky-haired picture on the wrapper.

"Please, suh, don't wrop up de com'." Maria grabbed that and stuck it among her wool. Then she strutted away, to the other women, and took no more notice of Jim. Jim refired his cigar and swelled with importance.

While Maria was gone, in a burst of generosity, Jim bought a string of blue beads for Jinny. This sent the child rushing away to show her mother. In quick succession he took the watch-chain for $2.75, plug tobacco fifty cents, a dime's worth of snuff, twenty-five cents' worth of chewing-gum in pink wrappers, drank two glasses of cider, purchased a pair of gloves for fifty cents and a huge bag of gingersnaps for fifty cents.

Maria drifted back as he was asking, "Lemme see one o' dem mouth harps."

The clerk handed it to him; he played a few snatches, grinned and acquired that for fifty cents. Jinny returned just as he ordered, "Six o' dem sardines."

Blinky tied up the sardines and held out his hand for more money while Jim dug deep into all his pockets, but every cent he could resurrect was that solitary silver dime. Jim stared at Maria and Maria stared back at Jim.

"Look a heah, Jim, is you done spent all o' dat money?"

"No, Maria, I ain't spent 'cept two or three dollars. I musser drapped it on de flo'." He got down on his knees and began to peer among the boxes, while Maria fetched a broom and swept—to no effect. Blinky footed up his sales memorandum.

"This makes $9.95 without the sardines—you ought to have ten cents left."

Jim arose: "Dat's all right den ef I ain't lost none of it. Come along, Maria; less go home." Her husband started in the lead of his procession, playing furiously on the harp.

Maria picked up the molasses jug. "Lawdy, Jim, dis jeg feels mighty light?"

"Never bought no molasses," he replied, and went on playing.

"Whar's de meat an' de meal?" Maria demanded.

"Never bought none."

"An' de coal oil, an' de coffee, an' de—" his wife

dropped the empty can and jug with a rattle, then grabbed hold of Jim's coattail.

"D'ain't a dust o' meal in de house, or a bite o' meat, or a drop o' molasses," she persisted desperately. "You ain't bought no rations—an'—an' I'm hongry."

Then Jim suddenly remembered that he, too, was hungry.

They sat down on a box side by side. "All de money's gone," said Jim.

"Tell me, Jim, what is you bought?"

He exhibited his purchases without enthusiasm, while Maria sprang up and confronted him, her arms akimbo. "Jim Fields, dem chillun—"

Jim waited for no more; he rose sheepishly, called Blinky Wilson into the back part of the store and held a whispered consultation.

"All right, Jim," the clerk agreed; "it's strictly against rules, you know, but we'll exchange the things for you. How much provisions do you want?"

Maria stepped into the breach and took charge of their trading; she called off the list of regulation rations. Blinky added up the items. "That's four eighty-five; now what do you want to trade back?"

Jim scratched his head and looked at Maria's comb; Maria glanced furtively at Jim's watch-chain, then both looked down at little Jinny hanging by her chin from the edge of the counter. Jim and Maria simultaneously reached for Jinny's beads and handed them back to the clerk. Jinny howled.

Jim cuffed her on one side and Maria on the other. "Shet up! Beads ain't no 'count nohow."

By the time Blinky had wrapped the packages, filled the molasses jug and oil can, they had only decided upon Jinny's beads as a sacrifice. Blinky piled up the provisions and tossed the beads into the case. "These were thirty cents. That leaves four fifty-five. What else do you want to trade back?"

Jim eyed Maria's comb, and Maria eyed Jim's watch-chain.

"Dat watch an' chain jes' makes it," she suggested, but Jim took her comb and laid it on the altar, with the gingersnaps and gloves.

"Leaves two-eighty," said Blinky. "What else?"

Jim followed the clerk's eye, but the chain glittered too brilliantly to be parted with; so he took Blinky into a far corner where none of the negroes could see him, and, after another consultation, slipped the watch into his hand.

"This leaves you twenty cents to the good," the clerk remarked.

Jim swaggered back to wife and child, flipping his watch-chain triumphantly. "Gimme one box o' sardines, a can of simon-fish an' a dime's wuth o' gingersnaps."

Maria packed their possessions away in the biggest basket, while Jim posed in the full glare of the light, so that his new watch-chain might dazzle the other negroes.

"Jinny, you tote de oil can," he said, and took up the molasses jug himself.

Then they departed. With a mouth full of gingersnaps Jinny forgot her beads, and Jim was playing "Old Aunt Jemima" on the harp.

V

THE LAZY MAN'S CROP

COTTON has been called "a lazy man's" crop because it can be worked at any old time or neglected at any old time. As Wash Johnson says, "Nothin' don't happen till it takes place nohow, an' dere's anudder day tomorrer which ain't touched yit."

His crop never seems to get its tail in a crack, like wheat, and require attention right now. When wheat is ripe it must be cut or lost, the most patient field will not wait for next week. The time for cutting is so short it might almost be measured in hours, and justifies the statement that before harvesting machinery was invented a single laborer, by hand, couldn't save enough grain to feed himself through the year.

It used to be, in happy-go-lucky times, that a traveler might drive through our country after Christmas and see thousands of acres still white with cotton when they should have been picked clean in November.

From the first plowing to its sale in the fall, the cotton crop formerly required about one hundred days of applied labor. This work was not done all at once, but doled out on the instalment plan.

47

For example: Wash Johnson and wife cultivate twenty acres. Early in the spring Colonel Woodville, having a half interest in their crop for rent and supplies, begins to nag at Wash to get the land plowed up.

"Yas, suh. Yas, suh," Wash promises. "Next week, suh. Next week."

Week after next when Wash can't stave it off another minute, he drags out a plow and attaches his mule.

"Ugh! Ugh! Dis sho is hard work. Hard."

Altogether, with interludes for recuperation, plowing and planting occupies twelve days, after which Wash reclines in the shade of a chinaberry tree and observes the green young cotton as it sprouts up from the ground. To observe is not fatiguing.

Grass and weeds are also growing and must be chopped out, cotton plants being thinned to a "stand." His wife helps, maybe some half-grown children, their shiny hoe blades glinting in the sunlight. Ten days cleans their crop and Wash is plum wore out.

"Ugh!" he groans, "Farmers sho do have tough times. I'd ruther be a bishop."

After the chopping Wash could lie flat on his back under the chinaberry tree for several weeks until the boss rouses him to "lay by." "Laying by" means to throw dirt against the roots of the plant for which Wash again leads out his protesting mule who drags a plow down the middles for twelve interminable days. "Now! Dat's done."

He has now sweated for thirty-four days and feels entitled to another few weeks' vacation, until picking time rolls around in August.

Any tenant, by a lick and a promise, can grow more cotton than he will pick. So in the fall his boss must import extra pickers, usually an idle class from nearby towns. This makes the plantation's annual festival, when high yaller gals and tantalizing browns arrive from Vicksburg with a flash of gold teeth to help Wash gather his crop. During that hectic period Wash has lady adventures all over the place, and wife trouble at home for fifty days, with dancing in the store at night, and crap games.

The fifty days of picking ought not to count as labor, but we add them to our previous thirty-four.

Hauling, ginning and selling—if Wash sells his own cotton—will consume twenty days, footing up a grand total of one hundred and four. That constitutes a year's work, an outside estimate. On many plantations ninety days of actual labor might be nearer the truth.

On these figures anybody's slate and pencil will demonstrate that Wash Johnson, after deducting fifty-two Sundays, has more than two hundred days which might be devoted to cows and pigs and chickens, with a kitchen garden on land that the boss gives him rent free. But Wash won't do that.

The fact is that nowhere else in the world can the peasant class earn a living with such economy of elbow grease. No agricultural laborer in other lands can supply the necessities of 365 days by putting in 104 days work, pay all his living expenses through the year and have cash money at Christmas. Clerks and salaried people in the cities cannot spend twenty-seven per cent of their time behind the counter and show three or four hundred dollars savings. Yet since the Civil War our cotton labor has done exactly that, and got away with it.

The negro has his point of view. One lone black man may be plowing in a field, while a dozen white loafers sit on the store gallery swapping yarns.

"Huh!" Wash grumbles. "Dere sets de white folks cussin' an' cussin' 'cause dese damn niggers won't work."

Times have changed since the boll weevil came, and farmers have to hustle. A planter of mathematical turn now gives these figures:

An acre of cotton contains seventy rows of two hundred and ten feet each, 14,700 lineal feet to the acre. Suppose Wash Johnson tends fifteen acres. To make his crop he must go over it twenty-two times. So that if Wash should travel on one straight line in a northeasterly direction from Memphis, Tennessee, knocking down stalks, plowing, dragging, chopping, cultivating, through Tennessee, Kentucky, West Virginia, Pennsylvania and New Jersey, then Wash would pick his last cotton boll just about the middle of Brooklyn Bridge. He must travel more than 900 miles on that fifteen acres.

VI

A SELF-SUPPORTING PROPERTY

SOME few people spoke of the weevil as a blessing in disguise while most farmers saw nothing except the disguise. Yet the pest accomplished wonders by compelling them to raise food, so if cotton failed they wouldn't starve. Thoughtful Southerners for generations had preached this doctrine, and county agents tried to teach diversification. "Feed yourselves, feed your stock," they pleaded, but nobody listened.

Dyed-in-the-wool old timers claim that they can buy corn cheaper than they can raise it. Here's the argument: an acre of cotton in a favorable season at high prices may gross one hundred dollars. The value of the corn on that same acre would be much less, therefore the planter buys corn and saves money. True on paper, but he can only buy corn out of his profits, and that planter is a rare bird who actually takes his cotton profit and lays in corn. No, he uses the cash for some urgent need, and when his mules get hungry he must outtalk a banker for the means to feed them. No farmer can outtalk a banker who's listening to the weevil; so necessity forced thousands of them to milk a few cows, to hatch chickens, and grow corn for their hogs.

51

As a pleasing interlude suppose we look at Prairie Plantation, where Great-great-grandfather Oldham had always done voluntarily those things to which the boll weevil drove his neighbors.

An Indian never laughs. His stolid countenance has no muscles of risibility. Yet even our unsmiling Choctaws considered that Manito the Mighty had jested with them by setting down a prairie in the midst of such tangled hunting grounds. There it lay, a stretch of open land surrounded by jungles and canebrakes so dense that Bruin himself could scarcely crash through. A fair bright glade contrasted with the gloom of murky swamps, and dark mysterious bayous were overhung by cypress trees. Sunshine glinted on the bodies of sleek deer; panthers slouched out from ambush and stalked them in long lush grass. Partridges whistled by day; owls hooted by night. And from the shores of demon-haunted sloughs came the cry of the mating wolf. Schools of sparkling minnows, in summer, flashed along the surface of secluded lakes that, in winter, would be covered by ducks and geese. No warrior need die to gain the happy hunting grounds.

It is not recorded how Great-great-grandfather Oldham had his attention first attracted to this country. Possibly he came here by accident to hunt with Choctaw friends, and built a hunting lodge on higher land fronting "The Bayou"—the same two-room structure of brick which now forms part of the family residence. Behind this lodge "the prai-

rie" unrolls its flat fertility, a patch of ground which
would cost him nothing to clear. At that period
(about 1816-1820) an occasional crude steamboat
went puffing down the Mississippi, then struggled
against its currents and tried to get back upstream.
Very possibly, however, Grandfather loaded his
slaves on a broadhorn, or keel boat, and floated them
down to what is now Friar's Point, marching two
miles inland. The prairie being ready for his plow,
he might produce a crop the first season.

About the time our state of Mississippi was admitted to the Union, in 1817, Grandfather Oldham
set to work, using the lodge as headquarters while
his blacks hewed out timbers and burned the brick
for cabin chimneys. That was the genesis of Prairie
Plantation. Five generations ago this shrewd old
pioneer began a battle with the wilderness that his
descendants have successfully carried on, though
thousands of others failed. The soil is the same as
that of adjoining properties—no difference in climate, weather, prices, or labor. Therefore, the difference between the profit and loss must lie somewhere else—perhaps in a system of management.

One day on this plantation the guest was shown
a battered ledger where, at the top of its first page,
the master had written his "ADMONITION TO
OVERSEERS AND MANAGERS." The paper
is stained, the ink has faded. His handwriting suggests vigor and precision, using the obsolete "double
ess" and a somewhat eccentric spelling. Long out

of style is this ancient book, yet its wisdom remains
sound; for here the master lays down his First Law
—to wit: before anything else be done, every overseer and every manager is required to produce a generous harvest of food for man and beast that cultivate the land. Hogs must be fattened on the corn,
mules grow strong on oats and hay, and man be fed
by all the kindly fruits of the earth. This was the
First and Great Commandment.

"And then," his stout old hand writes on—"and
then cotton." Then the master would grow a money
crop.

Through five generations of change and chance,
Prairie Plantation has farmed upon this principle
and kept out of debt, while neighboring plantations
followed the fetish of cotton, cotton, nothing but cotton, and were smothered beneath their obligations.

Life then was life in a land of simple living. Men
and women worked to live, instead of toiling at a
great commercial industry, as the production of fibre
for the world has since become. If Grandfather
Oldham had possessed a million dollars cash, during
much of the year he could buy nothing with it. Four
mules and a wagon were unable to haul a single
pound of meat from the steamboat landing. His
wheels would bog up in the swamp and Grandfather
must dig them out when summer came. The little
community, possibly half a dozen whites and forty
blacks, found itself, for months at a time, cut off from
communication with mankind, so that transporta-

tion impossibilities compelled the planter to do exactly what economic impossibilities will again force upon him—to live at home and board at the same place.

Grandfather could not import supplies. Whoever craved bacon and eggs for breakfast must feed his pigs and encourage his hens, weave his own cloth or run naked, make his own hat or raise freckles, tan his own leather for shoes or go barefoot like a duck. All hands contributed to supply their natural wants; the master riding his fields, the mistress at home with her sewing women, her dairy and smokehouse. Whites and blacks made themselves comfortable. Soon they had something that resembled a road along the bayou banks. Attorneys came. A county courthouse. Race horses. Poker games. Camp meetings. The plantation continued to be self-supporting as long as the master could lay down his First Law and enforce it.

The Civil War destroyed him and threw his labor into chaos. When peace came his descendants built up again on the same basis of self-support, for Grandfather Oldham's "Admonitions" were still the law. The then owners of Prairie Plantation were no longer slave-masters, yet more or less directed and influenced their free black tenants, while providing for themselves at the Big House practically everything that the white family consumed. Through the transition from slavery to freedom, Prairie Plantation survived and kept clear of debt. Then came a

frenzy of inflation and high prices following the
World War when swampers, white and black,
thought they had the world by the tail, forever and
ever, amen. Negro tenants, their pockets bulging
with yellow-backed currency, speeded about the
country in high-powered cars, drinking soda pop and
chunking bottles along the road.

Share-croppers strutted like millionaires. Old
Black Nancy had made her killing and an automobile salesman wanted his rake-off, using the bait of
a shiny flivver. No, sir-ree. No flivver for Nancy.
She desired nothing less than a big car like the
planter's wife. And Nancy bought her big car for
spot cash.

Flush times. White folks threw their money at
jay birds only a little less crazily than negroes. Cotton lands soared to speculative figures. A small
farmer with forty acres made fine profits and bought
the adjoining 400 acres on credit. Grew a bumper
crop and added 4000 more—with a mortgage. He
pyramided like a crap shooter, so that one crop
failure broke him flat.

In 1934 fine cars by the hundreds, belonging to
negroes as well as whites, were left out in the weather
to rust because nobody had money for licenses or gas.

When all about them went mad, someway or other
the people of Prairie Plantation retained a sem-
blance of sanity and stubbornly followed the First
Law as laid down in Grandfather's ledger, so that

the original owners continue to own it—without a mortgage.

Against this sketchy background of what happened to big plantations we may now take stock of Prairie in the growing season of 1934. Ten miles of highroad, long since improved from a streak of mud, is of gravel, wide and smooth enough to permit a speed of sixty. In fields at our left, sturdy young cotton has grown six inches high, its long straight rows made by a tractor and cleanly cultivated. Under governmental restrictions, all the land is not planted to cotton. More corn than anybody ever saw now waves its fronds of vivid green in exact parallelograms. Large areas of oats are turning brown, almost ripe for the thresher. And lovely patches that flaunt the purple blossoms of the vetch.

As a novelty in this land of cotton, every negro cabin has a new fence of cypress pickets, and wire netting to rabbit-proof their gardens. Each garden fence tells its story of persistent ding-donging by a manager to make Wash Johnson grow his own vegetables. Wash is a free person of color, fast black, to whom the boss gives a truck patch without rent, gives him the seed, and then stands by to be sure that the seed is actually planted. Through the spring and summer, regularly as he inspects his own crops, the boss must watch to see that Wash's cabbages and peas do not perish from neglect. When winter comes, he must keep a vigilant eye upon that fence; otherwise Wash Johnson will burn those pickets. Of course, Wash need only stroll a few yards to the big timber and cut all the fallen limbs that he wants, but the fence is more convenient.

As a sign that prosperity has turned our corner, we see on the highway an occasional flivver that backfires and sputters toward us, jammed full of the Black Hope. Which means that negroes are earning a little from day labor. They stop at a filling station, take up a collection among themselves and buy three gallons of gas with a pint of oil. When gas runs out, they walk.

Nothing tickles a colored person like "ridin' in a Fode." Here comes the family in its rickety relic that groans and rattles. A grinning negro boy is steering, his little sister beside him, while another black girl stands on the running board. All of them are laughing because daddy has got their mule hitched in front, towing them to the store.

Wherever the white folks live is called the Big House, whether it be large or small. The first Big House on Prairie was burned long ago, and nobody knows what it looked like. The present residence stands well back from a plantation road, concealed by a fringe of trees. To reach it, we cross a cotton field and enter at the open gates, then follow a winding driveway among oaks that dot the smooth-mown lawn.

It is not a mansion and makes no pretense to lordliness. The sun gleams slantwise on a low Greek portico, flanked by pergolas whose whiteness is embowered in greenery and blossoms. Two rooms on the left, one behind the other, with a hall between, were once the hunting lodge of Grandfather Oldham, solidly built of bricks. To this sturdy structure other rooms have since been added.

About the place there clings a flavor of the Old South, its ease, its graciousness of living, like half-imagined whiffs of lavender; yet a South that's wholly practical, the New brought up to date and adapted to modern needs without destroying what was good in the Old.

Glance at the ancient dairy in the rear, located very near the residence, for Grandmother must make every step count. Dumpy and squat, fifteen feet square, its bricks were burned on this property and laid by slaves. Grandmother couldn't procure ice to keep her milk and butter fresh, so evaporation was created by a trench of running water that flowed all around her dairy on the inside. When refrigeration became available, the obsolete dairy was abandoned and a tall brick chimney erected which converted it into a furnace room to heat the residence.

Prairie has new barns with the latest conveniences, yet there's one old timer that may outlast them all. Its center is of squared cypress logs, mortised and fastened together with wooden pins. This veteran may still be serviceable after more recent buildings have rotted down.

The altered status of labor makes a vital difference between Yesterday and Today. Before the

Civil War, Grandfather could parcel out the work of his people, assign so many to the cornfield, so many to the oats. He had shepherds for the sheep, hog-masters for the pigs, and a veterinarian to keep his animals healthy. Trained gardeners provided their green food, while old women tended their chickens, ducks and geese. Guineas tended themselves. Our planter can't do that now, he manages as best he may. Grandfather never spent one single penny for meat, and present plantations could now supply their tenants just as bountifully if Wash Johnson hadn't "sot his head agin it."

Rations are issued on every other Saturday at the store, in a fixed allowance. The negro will buy anything that he can get on credit, but in bad years planters hold them down to strict necessities. On ration day, tenants flock around the commissary, chattering as happily as blackbirds. The Al Fresco Beauty Shoppe is a featured attraction for colored gents to have their kinks marceled. They make a gala occasion in the dance hall, where a perfumed " 'fessor" thumps a piano that sounds like brickbats pelting a tin roof. At the rear, behind a screen, is the crap table on which dead-game sports may plunge a nickel's worth. In the adjoining store, the manager already has their doles weighed out and sacked for quick delivery. This is the only place on earth for Wash to get a pair of galluses or a bite of chow. Nevertheless, he often refuses the very same bacon that's served to appreciative guests at the Big House.

Most of our planters are now making earnest efforts to provide their own food, which they eat themselves, while negroes grumble. In prosperous years, when there was a keen competition to get and hold their labor, no plantation owner dared to issue home-cured meats. His tenants would move, leaving him with fields to grow up in weeds. Now they have nowhere to go, for nobody wants more labor; yet Wash Johnson continues to obstruct the path of plantation economy.

Tenants raise the same objection to canned goods put up at home. Our soil produces rosy tomatoes, succulent roasting ears, okra, beans, peas, berries, peaches—everything. On a bright June morning you may see the mistress at Prairie Big House out in her yard under a tree, with tables full of cans, preserving her winter food. Competent negro women help at the job and receive a generous share. Then, here's what happens—invariably happens:

The mistress put up dewberries—dozens and dozens of cans—of which Aunt Hannah toted home her liberal portion. That evening Hannah fancied a dewberry pie, but she would not waddle across the road and pick her berries ripe from a bush. Not much, Hannah wouldn't, not when she could repose in her rocking-chair and open a can. So the mistress will have dewberry pastries at Valentine's Day while Hannah's are gone before Thanksgiving.

Some planters consider it practicable to establish a community garden, especially at a time when everybody has idle land. As was uniformly done before the Civil War sufficient acreage might be devoted to vegetables, which the cotton negro has plenty of leisure to cultivate. But here we strike the same old snag: Wash Johnson won't do that, even in a crisis of acute distress. And in prosperous seasons there wouldn't be a Chinaman's chance for him to prank with garden truck when he can step on the gas.

Early settlers in our delta found water to be one of their knottiest problems. At first they dipped it up from stagnant bayous that were foul with decaying vegetable matter. Then they had a roof, a rain barrel and a plank gutter to catch the drip. Underground cisterns—huge sunken jugs of brick and cement—proved unsatisfactory because Mississippi River overflows would fill them with mud. Artesian wells now furnish a flow of pure water, and houses are so thoroughly screened against mosquitoes that they have practically got rid of malaria. In Grandmother's time, if she wanted to give a party, she must reckon with the "chill day" of her cronies. On Sundays, Sally couldn't come, and Maria would be shaking on Thursdays. Hester was laid up every Tuesday. Silly as this sounds, it was true. Now we have less malaria along the Mississippi River than is reported along the Hudson. Screens and artesian wells have turned the trick.

"Howdy, Sis Ida," says Parson Wiggins as he drapes himself across her gate. "Sis Ida, de boss is done dug hisself one o' dem artillery wells."

"Dere now," his fat parishioner grunts, "you say he is?"

"Sholy. An' sont dat water off to git scan'alized. An', Sis Ida, lemme tell you. Dat artillery water is nigh 200 per cent hydrophobia."

For commercial wheat, delta lands cannot rival the Northwest, yet at a pinch Prairie Plantation may eat its own flour. During the World War, the United States Government feared a shortage and asked our farmers to grow breadstuffs. Prairie withdrew a considerable acreage from cotton and sowed the grain. Had luck. It throve, but the harvesting required an outlay of more than five thousand dollars for machinery. Although mistakes were made, the plantation stored up quantities of wheat which could not be shipped because of a freight-car famine. The Government took none of the product, so the planter ground it at home. Pretty good flour, whole wheat, unbolted. The plantation was smothered in flour, buried under mountains of flour, choked with flour which they were unable to sell. The Big House ate sponge cakes, batter cakes, layer cakes, rolls, pop-overs, pies, hot biscuits and cold light bread, but Wash Johnson refused to touch it as part of his rations. He insisted upon having white flour—"store-bought stuff"—and the whole-wheat flour found no market.

After taking their loss without a murmur, they sold five thousand dollars' worth of machinery for junk.

Let an intelligent stranger go through the country today and he'll get an impression of practical patriotism, with no Fourth-of-July bunk.

Everywhere our people are considering their situation—at the one-horse farmer's fireside, at the country store, the banks—are even daring to speak aloud of heresies that never before have been whispered: "Suppose our Cotton Belt should stop fighting for supremacy in markets of the world? Instead of continuing our efforts to clothe mankind at prices that keep us impoverished, might it not be wiser to plant only for our own spinners in America, and let the international market get its supplies elsewhere?"

This state of mind is not mentioned either to defend or refute, but merely to illustrate how our South is casting about and weighing the possible effect of all contingencies.

Southerners are thinking more earnestly, and thinking more nationally, as to what seems best for the whole country. If every big planter, every small farmer and every Wash Johnson should produce—as he undoubtedly can produce—his own foodstuffs, what would become of Northwestern farmers with their wheat, corn, oats and hay? Feeding ourselves might become a boomerang, for if the South no longer buys from other sections of this Union, how can we sell our cotton to them? Part of the answer—a selfish part—lies in the fact that the South can feed itself, while the North cannot clothe itself.

The plantation negro forms a curiously sentimental factor in our predicament—one that cannot be worked out in terms of dimes and dollars. Because of the plowing up of 1933, with drastic reductions of acreage under the Bankhead Bill, we have so much vacant land that one planter tells me he has sixty families that he does not need. Yet the negroes continue to occupy his cabins, and he must find a way to provide their maintenance. If these helpless people were put off his property, where would they go? No other planter wants them, and they are fit for nothing except cotton. Look at old Aunt Sally, sick and sitting on her gallery; the planter cannot turn her out, and will not.

At the beginning of things, Prairie Plantation was an isolated community that could live apart from the world, remote and self-sufficient. The remoteness now is gone. It's just a few steps to the telephone, and company runs out for a game of contract or afternoon coffee, with a chat upon the porch. Friends reach the plantation with less delay and annoyance than if it were in New York City. Twenty-five miles over excellent roads is not so far as five miles on Manhattan; no red lights, no traffic jams, no football tactics in the subway.

Dinner guests assemble round a table quite correctly set; lights, napery, dishes and service being little different from any well-ordered city home. The men and women, however, may prove far more interesting.

Table talk drifts hither and yon, like leaves that are tossed around on gusts of laughing wind—new plays, politics, books—with the ease and graciousness of our Old South.

What we are getting at is this: a complete answer to farmers who growl that if they fool with vegetables and chickens they'll have no time to ramble in their cars and go to picture shows. For more than a century, Prairie Plantation has tinkered with garden sass and setting hens, and has churned its own butter. During that time the property has survived a devastating war. It has risen out of recurring submergence by the Mississippi River. Overcoming drought and starvation prices, it has sent successive sons and daughters to the best schools of America and Europe. The boll weevil could not stop this soil from showing profits. Only once has the plantation been pledged to make a crop, and subsequent financial panics have laid no mortgage upon the land.

Through lean seasons and fat seasons, there it stands, a serene old sign-board pointing to what may happen if other farmers follow Great-great-grandfather Oldham's First Law: "Feed yourself, and then plant cotton."

VII

THE LUCK OF PANTHER BURN

Times is gittin' better now,
Which makes us niggers grin
Whilst pickin' out our cotton
An' haulin' to de gin.

De lint flies up all soft an' white,
Dem seeds dey draps like hail,
Ontil de ginner wrops it tight
An' rolls you out yo' bale.

"Here, Jake," de cunnel sorter smiles
An' pays me half.   Dat's fine.
Ain't had a nickel in my pants
Since nineteen twenty-nine.

Us tenants hangs aroun' de gin
An' laughs when cotton's high,
Den brags de biggest kind o' brags
'Bout what us aims to buy.

I'll stuff my mouf wid ginger snaps,
A barrel full o' pop;
Eat forty cans o' sardine fish
An' settle from de crop.

Jes' watch us niggers ride some more,
Tanks sloshing gasoline,
'Cause seed what used to sell for four
Is done hit seventeen.

COTTON! The magic name conjures up a vision of fluffy whiteness that matches the pure magnolia blossom and mingles with languorous perfumes of Cape Jasmine. Cotton! We see the "suth'n cunnel, suh," as cartooned on stage and screen, with drooping mustache and wide-brimmed panama, who sips a fragrant julep, while his lady's crinoline swishes through the great cool hallways of their colonnaded mansion.

Cotton! Happy negroes pick and sing in the fields. Teamsters are hauling to the gin. Black faces perch high upon wagonloads of new-gathered lint, like tar-balls set against a mountain of snow. Cotton! Fiery cavaliers race their thoroughbreds. Stakes at poker tables mount to dizzy heights. Ruined aristocrats. The punctilious Code Duello. Gorgeous carriages deposit guests for revelry at the Big House. At the doors of humble cabins fat old mammies tend their pickaninnies, who wallow in the dust. Cotton! Banjoes and bandannas, coonjine dances and crap games.

That's the standard romance of cotton, but sounds like rot to me.

Anyhow, it's gone. Crinoline has gone and gasoline has come. Yet the fable held some grain of truth. Forty years ago the lives of white men and black men were much simpler in our marvelously fertile delta that stretches like a flat green floor between Memphis and Vicksburg. Life was easy. They took it easy. With all due reverence, the planter regarded himself as a partner of Almighty God. And relied upon his partner. The Lord will provide; the Lord had already provided thousands of fecund acres that supported the old-time landlord. The Lord sent His tepid rains and germinating sunshine to sprout the seed. Young cotton popped up overnight, flourished, bloomed and bore abundant harvests. Negroes gathered the colonel's crop. Managers attended to the shipment. A factor paid his drafts. Now and again the factor's lawyer drew another mortgage. No trouble, no worry. The colonel need only sign it, then catch a steamboat with his family for the Saratoga races.

Our pioneering grandfathers found plenty of toilsome labor in clearing and civilizing this delta. High water, mosquitoes, malaria, gun-fighting and outlaws and bad roads kept them rustling until these enemies were finally conquered. Then followed a breathing space for their sons, during which the landlord might lounge on the front porch of his plantation store, with both feet propped against its banister and enjoy an after-breakfast cigar.

Negro tenants winked craftily at one another and whispered, "Ef you 'quires sump'n, wait till de Cunnel smokes up half 'o his seegyar. Dat throws him in a yieldin' humor an' yo' wants will den be justified." So old black Jerry eyed his boss from behind a barn, then came shambling up the store steps and grinned.

"Mornin', Cunnel. Trouts is strikin' in Tangle Lake."

"Yes, Jerry. I'll give 'em a riffle tomorrow. Seine me some minnows."

"Sho will, Cunnel. Sho will."

That opens their negotiations and by cunning approaches Jerry maneuvers to his point, "Cunnel, I needs a ham."

"But, Jerry, you got one Saturday."

"Dat's de troof, Cunnel, de Gawd's troof. An' dat ham wouldn't be all et up ef so many niggers hadn't swarmed at my house an'—"

Jerry's crop was badly in the grass and would never pay for rations that he had already got on credit, nevertheless his glib tongue outtalked the boss.

"All right. Root around back yonder and dig up a ham for yourself. Clerk's gone to town. Nobody here but me."

As the negro trudges off with twelve pounds of toothsome delicatessen, the planter finishes his cigar. If he hasn't already forgotten the transaction, he may jot down on a scrap of paper, "One ham, Jerry King," then file that charge item in his accounting department, which consists of a cracker box stowed away underneath his counter. Or he may be too busy to get up and merely mark "one ham" on the white-washed post beside him. Sometimes the colonel used a nice clean shingle as a daybook, which served very well unless somebody happened to split up that shingle for kindling.

This slosh-along system had its virtues. Even now, in memory, certain figures stand out as patterns of cultured gentlemen, public spirited, generous, genial, tolerantly courteous toward all men and respectful to every woman. High standards of honor and an unbought grace of life made the world far sweeter for their presence.

One by one those men went broke.

Panther Burn Plantation typifies a different kind of planter and a modern system. Negligent farmers speak about "the luck of Panther Burn." It's not luck. The property has shown more profits in good years and lost less when crops were poor, because of business management. The boss keeps track of every detail as this scrap of conversation proves.

"Here! Mister Johnny-come-lately, pay 'tention to Uncle Joe." The veteran black tenant checked his mule at a turnrow and warned the new hand: "Don't try none o' yo' tricks. Us got a boss what knows de birthday of ev'y mule on Panther Burn."

"Say he do? Knows de mules' birthdays? How come?"

"He knows ev'ything, an' den some mo'! Got a machine in de office which tells him. Dat white man keeps count o' how many plugs o' tobacker you chaws. Ef Dr. Smith comes to see you fer colic, our boss puts colic down on his machine. Ef yo' wife has a baby, dat machine tells him 'boy' or 'gal,' as de case mought be."

These two garrulous darkies, gossiping in the field, pretty nearly sized up Panther Burn Plantation, where nine thousand open acres are being cultivated with the promptitude and accuracy of a banking corporation. Its bosses scrutinize the minutest detail.

Panther Burn has always been looked upon as a pattern in the Delta. Its former owner, Captain John Willis, made the name a synonym for success and square dealing with negroes. When other planters are scraping around for labor to fill their vacant cabins, this enormous place never lacks a tenant. Year in and year out their operations make money—or did until the overwhelming year of 1931. Through wet season or dry, low prices or high, overflows or financial crashes, Panther Burn's books showed a profit. Even during the disaster of 1930, balances kept consistently on the right side of their ledgers.

The owners are practical men of long experience and sound judgment, who think out a policy. Then everybody—manager, storekeeper, ginner and tenant —pulls together.

Panther Burn is not a mere plantation; it's a principality, wonderfully prolific, whose mellow miles lie along the banks of Deer Creek. Seven hundred black families live and labor here—1700 "head" as the negroes put it, counting men and women, big and little. And seven hundred mules. Stores, gins, blacksmith shops, a residence street for white employees, railroad station, post office and churches form a busy community, with its own school district where 350 black children are instructed.

Four white managers supervise all planting operations, each having his separate fields for which he's held responsible. New ground is annually being added, more and more cotton produced. In ten years production increased from 1426 bales to 5940.

Tenants are divided into two classes: the "renters," consisting of thrifty negroes that own their mules and gear. To these will be assigned as many acres as their families and hired hands are able to cultivate, for which the "renter" pays a fixed rental—seventy pounds of lint cotton per acre. "Share hands" own no stock, nothing except their hides and legal clothes to cover them. They are given land, cabin, mules, gear, everything, then split fifty-fifty with the landlords.

While Panther Burn has perhaps a higher percentage of intelligent negroes than most plantations, yet tenants and share hands alike need the daily direction of white men. In varying weather, on diverse soils and with different seed, nearly every negro must be shown how and when to work his crop.

To show him is the job for a trained agriculturist. The manager must know. He consults the boss, four managers confer with one another and see that things are properly done.

Any manager sufficiently competent to be retained year after year on Panther Burn must understand his business; and, furthermore, he must by some sort of instinct sense the negro psychology. Many a planter fails because he cannot get results from his labor. Some are too hard, many more are too lenient. The negro is a shrewd judge of white men and gives willing obedience to those who treat him fairly. But if any Panther Burn tenant or share hand refuses to cultivate his crop as directed, the landlord simply takes a loss and moves him off the property.

Frederick the Great once said, "An army goes on its belly." So does a plantation, and Panther Burn's service of supplies clicks like a clock. From early spring a regiment of human beings must eat, drink and wear clothes on credit, until cotton turns into money about September 1st. Seven hundred mules standing idle at the trough will eat themselves up in a year.

The pockets of a cotton-farming negro may bulge with money at Christmas, yet before the first of February it has vanished for gasoline and gingersnaps, so the boss begins issuing rations on credit. There's the rock where many a planter has been wrecked. If the season looks promising he allows his tenants too much latitude at the store. The crops fail and he loses all.

Heretofore Panther Burn tenants and share hands

were supplied with actual commodities. To subsist
a family of three, this standard ration was issued
every two weeks:

16 pounds dry salt meat	$1.92
8 pounds lard	1.20
24 pounds flour	.75
24 pounds meal	.60
5 pounds rice	.30
1 gallon molasses	.80
2 plugs tobacco	.30
Salt	.05
Coffee	.35

Epicures would consider it a skimpy menu, but
the negro may supplement his store rations by growing greens in the garden patch to cook with salt meat.
He may wax fat on cabbages, potatoes, all sorts of
truck which the soil produces most generously.
Busy hens should supply omelets. Pasture lands,
free of rent, encourage him to keep a cow. His hog
pen too is free. The slightest exertion gives him
fruit.

Their lesson has been partially learned. Every
planter is now dinning, dinning, dinning at his
tenants, and everywhere new fences are being built
for kitchen gardens, for pigsties and hen-houses.
Store stuff is cut to the minimum, and negroes are
compelled to do what they should always have done
from choice.

Here's one case: Steve Jackson, Senior, has five

grown boys, a wife, daughter and cousin to help him work. Fifty-five acres of cotton, and twenty-three acres are planted in corn with beans to grow upon the stalk, and give back to the land what the corn takes out.

  5 acres in soy beans for stock feed and hay
  ½ acre of cow peas for table use
  ¾ acre sweet potatoes
  ¼ acre tobacco for smokes and "twist"
  1 acre Louisiana sugar cane for molasses
  ½ acre sorgum cane
  ¼ acre Irish potatoes
  ⅛ acre peanuts
  1 acre kitchen garden, cabbages, onions, peppers, collards, tomatoes, all sorts of green food
  2 cows, 13 head of hogs. Plenty of chickens
  12 or 15 acres of free pasture, fenced in

Old Steve and family, like most of Panther Burn negroes, can live pretty well, and owe very little at the end of the year.

It has long been a rule on Panther Burn never to buy stock feed. Fancy figures for cotton will seduce many a planter to increase his yield by devoting every acre to lint and raising no corn, on the theory that a successful cotton acre brings cash enough to purchase more grain than can be grown on two acres. Panther Burn, however, sticks to the live-at-home idea, one third of its acreage being planted in alternate hills of corn and soy beans. Added to green

stretches of alfalfa, upward of two thousand five
hundred are growing feedstuffs. Next year these
lands will go back to cotton and the crops be rotated.

Partly because of 1930's disaster and worse in
1931, the plantation has changed its service of supplies. Instead of doling out meat and meal and
molasses, the bosses have adopted a "cash limit" system. Every other Saturday all tenants and share
hands assemble at the store, where the head of each
family is given a small envelope of cash. This is
based upon 75 cents per acre per month, so that a
negro whose wife and children help him to cultivate
thirty acres will receive on "limit day" an advance
of $11.25. He gets no further credit and pays cash
at the store. The store is extremely well handled,
wholly independent of the plantation. All plantation purchases are charged up and their merchandise
must show a separate profit.

The store too is somewhat of a bank. Here and
there a prudent negro saves his money, which he
leaves there on deposit, drawing four per cent interest.

In the wolfishness of modern competition, he that
produces the best commodity, produces it more
cheaply and sells with more wisdom is the man that
will survive. Agricultural experts of Panther Burn
are always experimenting with new seed and new
methods to develop the very highest grade and staple
that can be grown. "Grade" refers to cleanliness,
freedom from dirt, trash and stains, while "staple"
signifies the length and strength of fiber. Cotton

will not year by year maintain its excellence. The fibre deteriorates. To produce only the best, Panther Burn buys many tons of fresh seed every season.

Careful handling pays big dividends. On settlement day black Wash Johnson discovers that his bale brings ten dollars more than Andy Elliott's bale, because Wash took more pains in picking.

An ignorant black man who plows a remote acre in Mississippi cannot comprehend that he's got himself all tangled up with the whirligig of politics, trade depressions and financial fluctuations of the earth. That negro trudges along his row, mumbling and wondering why ten bales one year make him rich, and fifteen bales another year won't let him pay license on a dilapidated flivver. But the boss must look ahead and try to understand, must confront the loss of old markets and seek new ones.

Panther Burn and allied properties have many thousand bales to sell. Suppose we trace one bale:

Wash Johnson, colored, helps to load 1500 pounds of seed cotton on a plantation wagon. This will yield 500 pounds of lint and 1000 pounds of seed. It goes through the gin, and Wash's brand new bale rolls out upon the platform. The bale is marked and tagged. Wash is given a memo of its number. Railroad or truck transports it to the company's headquarters at Leland, Mississippi, where the bale is sampled and expert classers determine its grade and staple.

The planting company immediately sells Wash

Johnson's bale to the marketing company at ruling quotations for that day. The marketing company is a subsidiary of Panther Burn, but operates independently of the plantation. The marketing company pays the planting company for Wash Johnson's bale, and Wash immediately receives a check at full price for his share. In a single season Panther Burn distributed among its tenants more than $275,000 cash for lint and seed. Which means that negro farmers, after paying their year's expenses, had that much clear money at Christmas.

A sample from Wash Johnson's bale is spread upon the marketing company's table, in a scientifically lighted room whose steel-gray walls show every speck of foreign matter in the lint. Side by side lie the samples from 199 other bales just like Wash Johnson's. This grade and staple exactly suits a certain spinner to whom Panther Burn has been selling the same cotton for many years. So they wire that spinner, offering two hundred bales of "Sally" at such a price. "Sally" is their "type," their symbol word which tells the spinner that those two hundred bales are strict middling 1⅜ staple.

At his end of the line the spinner knows that "Sally" will class out as described, every bale of uniform grade and staple, precisely what his machinery is adjusted to handle. There'll be no wrangles over "Sally," no rejections, no arbitration at the New York Cotton Exchange. For that assurance the spinner is willing to pay a stiffer price.

The big planter has an advantage in selling his crop because he can supply certain mills with their entire raw material. A small farmer may be unable to sell five bales, while Panther Burn finds a ready market for five hundred.

The brain behind this harmonious organization is that of the "Big Boss," and he knows exactly what goes on. Every employee cooperates. By intelligent cultivation they produce the very best cotton, spending thousands of dollars to improve its grade and staple, and not one penny is lost in extravagance or waste. For the highest type of cotton a competent sales force gets the highest price. And that's the simple answer to Panther Burn's success.

For 1931, Panther Burn's cost of production— taxes, overhead, supplies—was based upon an expected price of 15 cents a pound yet millions of bales were actually sold below 6 cents. Of course the plantation lost money. During 1932 its owners followed the course of prudent business and cut expenses to the bone. Tenants pretty well fed themselves and kept their mules looking slick.

What lies in the future nobody knows. But if the South continues to grow cotton it must be done on business principles. Slipshod methods are gone, the poetry of the pageant is gone, and landlords can no longer keep books on a shingle.

VIII

THE ONE-HORSE FARMER SELLS

THE small white farmer brings seven or eight bales to market every fall and cannot have a selling organization like Panther Burn. He peddles it himself and produces the bulk of our American crop, possibly 75 per cent.

There's no hired help on his little "place," only the wife and barefoot children. After their family teamwork has gathered enough for a couple of bales, the farmer hauls it to a public gin, or that of some nearby planter who does extra work for neighbors. In the gin hopper seed go one way, rattling like hail, and soft lint flies another way until a bale is packed and rolled out of the press, wrapped in jute bagging and bound with six iron ties. The bale is four and a half feet high as it stands on the platform, four feet wide and twenty-seven inches thick. It weighs, we will say, exactly five hundred pounds.

His rickety wagon will haul only two bales which he loads at the gin and sets out for town where he does his "trading" with a merchant that furnishes supplies. The law would not permit him to go anywhere else because the merchant holds a deed of trust on his growing crop, and this cotton represents his sole means of payment.

When the farmer reaches town he drives into a warehouse, dumps off the cotton and has it weighed. The weigher is a person of long experience, trusted by the community. He feels the bale and knows how much moisture it has soaked up and what honest allowance should be deducted.

The warehouse clerk issues a receipt giving the weight, and pulls a sample of cotton by cutting a hole in the bagging and drawing out several ounces of lint. Each sample, showing the grade and staple, is put up separately in a stiff paper cornucopia, so when the grower sets out to get bids, a buyer knows that he has deposited in the warehouse 1000 pounds of strict middling cotton 1⅛ staple.

The merchant is glad to see him bring two bales which means that part of the customer's supply account will be paid, and money's getting tight at this season of the year. Prices hover around 11½ cents; newspapers print daily quotations, and the farmer also listens to market reports that come every morning over a radio in the country store. So he knows what his cotton should sell for.

The merchant bids 11.55, then the farmer tries some "cotton buyers," representing larger firms in cities who make a business of collecting cotton and assembling it into "lots" of even-running grade and staple.

In making his round of buyers, the farmer carries the sample and warehouse receipts from which the buyer knows exactly what he's bidding on, and the best offer is 11.62 from a shipper who has an order for that type of cotton.

The farmer gives up his warehouse receipt and gets a check for $116.20 after the buyer has inspected both bales and drawn new samples. That closes their trade. The farmer, being trusted by his merchant, goes back to him with the check to apply on debts, and is allowed to retain a little cash.

It often happens that a merchant takes the cotton of customers who owe him and credits their accounts at ruling quotations, so the merchant who has a hundred customers becomes a considerable seller, exhibiting samples on his tables where buyers "class" them and make offers.

The buyer, having bought these two bales, adds them to others of like grade and staple until he fills up a hundred-bale lot which he has contracted to deliver to a certain mill. No actual money passes, everything is on paper. At the beginning of the season most buyers arrange a line of credit with the bank based on some money of their own as a margin. He gives the farmer a check, and that night protects his check at the local bank by depositing warehouse receipts against as many bales as he has purchased during the day. The bank holds the receipt as collateral, knowing that the actual bale is in the warehouse, and the buyer's margin is supposed to cover fluctuations of price. Everybody watches the market and if values decline, the bank frequently puts a buyer on the spot for more security.

The buyer sells this cotton to a spinner, say, at Providence, Rhode Island. Before being shipped to New England or exported, a "gin" bale," as it is called, must be compressed so that the freight car or vessel may carry twice as much in the same space. Powerful machines reduce the gin bale to about half of its original cubic contents.

After the cotton is loaded on freight cars, the buyer exchanges his warehouse receipts for a bill of lading which certifies that 100 bales are now in possession of the railroad for delivery. He then goes to the bank and draws a sight draft on the mill that bought the cotton, attaching his bill of lading. The mill treasurer must pay the draft before he gets the cotton. It's a cash transaction. The cotton goes forward by freight, the draft by mail. The New York bank returns the proceeds of the draft to the local bank which credits the buyer.

Formerly, before the cotton trade became so concentrated in the hands of a few big firms, progressive buyers from the South went to New England every August, visiting spinners for whom they bought raw material season after season. By personal contact they kept in touch with mill requirements and knew what quality of staple would be needed.

Revolutionary changes have shaken the trade since American spindles shifted nearer to southern fields. Railroads handle less and less cotton, much of which moves by truck for distances of two hundred and fifty miles. Concrete highways make it easy to carry the original "gin bales," saving cost at compress and warehouse.

The farmer in debt is not a free agent, neither is the merchant, the buyer, or the banker when cotton is dumped on the market all at once, more than the needs of mankind will absorb. Out of this condition grew the movement for cooperative selling.

By the middle of August millions of money are tied up in a growing crop, not a nickel coming back, and country bankers sail close to the wind. They have loaned to factors who finance farmers, loaned to merchants who supply farmers, and grub-staked the farmers themselves. To get this money local banks borrow in New Orleans, Houston, Atlanta; and larger institutions by lending all over the South find themselves hard pressed. Commercial wheels are clogged because cotton has not begun to move. Metropolitan financiers urge their correspondents to realize on the crop. New York calls up New Orleans, New Orleans wires Vicksburg; the Vicksburg banker phones the merchant; the merchant hollers for the farmer to haul some cotton. The farmer speeds up his picking; the ginner turns out a few bales, and the grower's mules trot off to town. The buyer gives him his check, the sight draft goes forward. Like that sweet old nursery rhyme, "The stick began to beat the dog, the dog began to bite the pig," until the pig jumps over the stile and everybody gets paid.

IX

COTTON EXCHANGES AND FUTURE TRADING

IF our farmer had hauled cotton to market in 1825, he must have sold on the wildest speculation, for neither merchant nor buyer could get news from Liverpool.

> England takes the surplus,
> And England makes the price.

For three months of that year New Orleans dealers twiddled their thumbs and waited the arrival of any vessel that might bring quotations. Nobody dared to trade for they could only guess what cotton was worth.

Nothing so demonstrates the improvement in world-wide facilities as the fact that today our one-horse farmer may stroll over to the cross-roads store and listen in on a radio.

"W.Q.B.C. speaking. Post Herald Station, Hotel Vicksburg." The announcer then gives Liverpool quotations, New York and New Orleans markets, weather reports, every scrap of information that affects the price of cotton. An isolated producer in the backwoods knows what his staple should bring, and knows it less than ten minutes behind the best-posted trader. Formerly a sharper might get advance tips and pick up country cotton below its value, a feat which has now become impossible.

No other commodity has such an organized staff of news gatherers to assemble statistics. Every mite of data is concentrated in cotton exchanges where a member need only glance at the blackboard to see whether São Paulo, Brazil, has got rain; pink-worm depredations in Egypt; or how many American bales were bought yesterday by the mills of Japan.

Before his eyes a member sees the government crop estimate, the world's visible supply and world consumption. It's all there for him to digest and form an opinion as to whether values will rise or fall. Busy clerks chalk up figures on the board which represent transactions in "spots" or "futures." Spots are actual cotton, the real stuff which is delivered when sold. Futures are sales for deferred deliveries, perhaps cotton sold in August on a contract to be delivered in December. When December comes, instead of the seller turning over 100 actual bales and the buyer receiving them, the parties may adjust their trade by payment of the difference in price.

Which means this: suppose the seller in August agrees to deliver one hundred bales of cotton in December at fifty dollars per bale, and suppose the quotations advance ten dollars per bale. According to an ancient British jingle, "Who sells cotton which isn't his'n, must buy it back or go to prison." The seller has no actual cotton and must buy in open

market, paying ten dollars more for each bale than
he contracted to sell for, so the buyer says, "Very
well, just give me one thousand dollars and we call
our deal square." Most future contracts are liquidated in this way.

Trades of this sort, usually for out-of-town clients,
are consummated by future brokers on the floor of
the Exchange. The old-time "spot broker," a go-
between in handling actual cotton, has practically
ceased to exist.

Periodically in this "land of the free and home of
the brave" we hear a howl about "gambling in
human necessities," and "speculators depressing the
price of agricultural products." "Vultures preying
on the vitals of our horny-handed sons of toil."
Popular stuff for a stump speech, and politicians
made the most of it.

Such complaints are not new. Egypt squawled
mightily when one of her progressive Pharaohs
hoarded all the grain for princely profits. Holland
turned black in the face because her tulips were "cor-
nered," and Spain raised sand over a tight little
squeeze in jackasses. Speculation is old, old, old,
and cotton has had its occasional spasm, but none
lately.

There's always a gambler in every market to bet
on prices going up, always a gambler to bet on prices
going down, and the paradoxical fact seems to be
that they enable legitimate business men to carry
through deals with a minimum of hazard.

If the mill treasurer buys a thousand bales of actual fibre to complete his contracts for cloth, he takes a chance that prices for raw material will not decline, unless he sells "futures" against the purchase. One trade offsets the other, and between them lies his gain.

The Southern buyer who agrees to ship the spinner one thousand bales at figures that show a neat margin, will immediately buy a thousand bales of futures. This, in both cases, is called "hedging" or "price insurance."

It is said that 85 per cent of conservative mill treasurers habitually pursue this hedging policy because they *do not want to gamble.*

In late August, Colonel Darius Woodville can pretty well estimate how many bales the Ruthven gin will turn out. By that time he also knows what his crop has cost, and December futures now sell on the board around 15 cents. At that price he can pay the bank for money loaned to feed Wash Johnson, and clip a substantial chunk off his mortgage.

Rarely does a planter admit that cotton might go lower, but Colonel Rye has been stung so often that he plays safe, and sells 600 bales of December contracts. Now he sits pretty and can't lose.

One of the greatest legal minds in America was that of Chief Justice Edward D. White. While a member of the United States Senate from Louisiana he said, "The question whether contracts for future delivery are valid contracts has been before the Supreme Court of the United States and courts of last resort in every state. Beyond all question it is as lawful to sell for future delivery as it is to sell for present delivery. They are both valid contracts."

A few years later the U. S. Supreme Court (Christie case, 198 U.S. 236) held that not only were these contracts legal but that they could lawfully be settled by either delivery or set off, that is by clearing one contract against another and paying only the balance due.

Canada also canvassed the problem in reference to wheat, and Sir Josiah Stamp reported. First: future trading benefits the farmer by furnishing a system of insurance for handling his product. Second: future trading furnishes the farmer an ever-ready and convenient means for marketing his product. Third: future trading furnishes a distinct benefit to the producer in the price that he receives.

X

THE BOLL WEEVIL

FOR fifteen years cotton had been struggling to recover from back sets of the Civil War, and to reorganize its industry on a basis of free labor. During the seventies, while panicky high prices declined, staple continued to sell at fair profits, and production steadily increased so that needs of the world were supplied. The South went through prosperous years and lean years, contending against the usual pests of plant life until the boll weevil made its appearance from Mexico in 1893. He was first heard of in the second year of our Civil War when a sudden infestation drove the peons from their cotton crop in the Monclova district of Mexico. After that we heard a-plenty of him, nearer and nearer, crossing the Rio Grande in 1893, and pushing into Texas. By 1905 the voracious beetle had invaded Louisiana; the Mississippi River delayed him only a few days. Tradition says that Mexican laborers brought them across the Rio Grande in filthy bed clothes, but they either flew over or swam the Mississippi on their own power.

This destructive insect, the only free-list importation that enters the South, does not masquerade as an article of consumption, being preeminently a consumer himself. The daintiest of all epicures, he eats nothing but cotton, and selects the choicest bits. He does not injure the plant itself, destroying only the fruit. A field grows up tall and gloriously green, but when the weevil gets through with it, one hundred acres may not yield a single bale.

A hungry brute is the weevil black
That preys on the cotton boll;
She breeds like fun in the summer's sun
And hides from the winter's cold.

She's a bill that bores like an augur sharp
And the daintiest taste has she;
Destroys the pod of its lint white heart
That maketh the clothes for me.

The negro plows with his flea-bit mule
Uprooting the cocklebur,
And the weevil knows that he sows and hoes
Preparing a meal for her.

The farmer may plant and sweat and pant
From dawn to sunset dim,
She gets there first ere the green bolls burst,
And there's nothing left for him.

Last year he made a bumper crop,
Paid every man his due,
But the weevil's snout has cleaned him out,
Ate crop and credit too.

The cotton plant stands from three to eight feet high, more like okra than anything else. Its blossom is yellow the first day, blushes to red and drops off, disclosing three tiny leaves which enfold the pale green globules no bigger than an English pea. This is the embryonic "boll" which is to produce the valuable lint. The boll swells out round and firm, somewhat smaller than an egg, gradually expanding until it turns brown, cracks open like a chestnut bur, and the staple is ready for picking. The sole value of a cotton plant lies in the boll. To this the farmer gives his undivided attention, and so does the weevil.

Mrs. Weevil isn't very big, only a quarter of an inch long, with a bill as long as herself which she knows how to use. When posing for her picture, she resembles a meditative baby elephant, barring a tail which is minus. She can walk, crawl, fly and swim, using every method of transportation; but it is her appetite and propagation that renders Mrs. Weevil most obnoxious.

If Mr. and Mrs. Weevil were cast into a cotton patch, lonely as Adam and Eve, they would immediately begin to populate the earth. Starting as utter strangers, fighting against poverty and social ostracism, they would rear a family of thirty millions before Jack Frost breaks up their maternity home. When her daughter attains the mature age of forty-three days, she helps mamma to breed.

Mrs. Weevil is an exclusive person and does not crowd her young. She lays an average of 139 eggs, but has been known to deposit more than 600, and prefers a separate square or boll for each one. One female will destroy fifty cents worth of cotton every time she takes a notion to increase her family. By some subtle instinct she can tell whether another Mrs. Weevil has already made an incubator of that particular boll, and if so passes on. If not, she punctures the boll, deposits her egg and proceeds to the next. This propensity makes her unpopular with the farmer, for a "stung" boll produces no cotton. The boll shrivels and dies while furnishing food for the growing worm. Later in the season Mrs. Weevil cannot be so fastidious, and lays her egg in the first boll she comes across.

The egg hatches into a white worm, develops, turns out a fine new bill, puts on wings and legs, then eats its way into the wide world ready for business.

The boll weevil stays at home until he has eaten all the squares and bolls on his own patch, then migrates to a neighboring cut of cotton and finally to another field or country. He's a good traveler, making forty miles a year.

When summer is gone Mrs. Weevil hides in the bark of a tree, curls up in the trash beside a hedgerow, or seeks out a knothole in a fence rail. The snuggest berth is the old cotton house which stands in every field. Its crevices and cracks form ideal winter quarters, where the weevil hibernates in the beetle or adult stage and requires no food. Millions of them die, birds search them out, but when all misfortunes have been reckoned with, a goodly number survive. These usually come from the latest brood that was hatched in summer.

Generally speaking, a cotton plant puts on three crops, bottom crop, middle crop, and top crop. If the season be long and favorable, a considerable amount of lint is produced by late blossoms which crown the top of the plant. The bottom crop grows rapidly, puts on squares faster than young weevil can consume them, and these may mature before the pest has multiplied in sufficient quantities to destroy. By the time the middle crop comes along, the weevils are ready to sting every immature boll. And there is no such thing as gathering a top crop if the field be full of weevil.

When Mrs. Weevil first located modestly in the good old U. S. A. near Brownsville, Texas, nobody paid her the slightest attention. She settled down and bred great-great-grandchildren whose activities roused the farmers to the fact that they were planting plenty of cotton and gathering none. The area of infestation extended eastward, steadily, almost on a fixed schedule of forty miles per year.

The Department of Agriculture at Washington saw this new menace that threatened our entire cotton belt, and immediately began a campaign of control where the weevil was already established, besides sending agents ahead of the pests to give warning. The agents held mass meetings, trying to make farmers prepare for what seemed inevitable. It is singular now to look back upon a fatuously indif-

ferent state of mind with which the official alarum
bell was heard. Farmers didn't believe a word.
Every man-jack of them who had a creek or rail
fence between himself and destruction, plugged
along in blind security, deriding the idea that the
pest would ever reach his acres.

Some planters got mad and said, "I don't believe
in spectacled professors galavanting around the
country preaching calamity and scaring our negroes.
Tain't the weevil but this infernal agitation that's
ruining us."

"Huh!" negroes commented among themselves.
"It's jest a trick o' dese white folks to keep from
givin' us niggers any grub."

Expert bugologists got busy studying the weevil's
history and habits. No candidate for public office
ever had his private life spied upon by so many different kinds of detectives.

During fifteen years of negligence the weevil continued to advance and consume. It spread from
Mississippi to Alabama, then marched through
Georgia like Sherman to the sea, and creating far
more havoc.

By 1922, 90 per cent of our cotton belt was over-
run. Everywhere she went Mrs. Weevil found the
same planting system, nothing but cotton; and everywhere she carried the same eating system, nothing
but cotton. People of uninfested districts refused to
take precautions, and planted an extra acreage in
cotton so as to be sure of an extra credit. Then the

weevil struck them. Farmers who had previously made three-quarters of a bale to the acre, now picked one bale to every thirty or forty acres, scarcely enough for seed. The planter with negro labor produced even less, and huge plantations grew up in cockleburs. Cabins stood empty.

Nothing seemed to stop or hurt the weevil. One old farmer sprang up at a scare meeting and shouted, "Tain't no sense tryin' to fight that devil. I corked up a lot of 'em in pure alcohol and kept 'em for two hours. They come out staggering drunk, and with a mighty good appetite. Then I sealed 'em in a tin can an' throwed 'em in my fire. When the can melted, them red-hot bugs flew out and burnt my barn."

To plant seed was worse than buying a lottery ticket, and cotton which had been so dependable as security was scratched from the list of pledges that would be received at any pawn shop. Planters who had jeered at spectacled professors couldn't raise a cent at the bank, and didn't know what to do, were unable to hold their labor without feeding them, and merchants refused to let them have more food.

During the spring of 1904, in certain sections of Texas, no man without reference to his previous financial status, could get a side of meat or a sack of flour on credit. So the Texas farmer planted vegetables, Irish potatoes, ribbon cane, corn, and raised hogs to eat. The State sustained fifty million dollars' worth of damage in one year, and its legislature wildly offered $50,000 reward for a remedy.

In part the remedy came of itself. The farmer's garden patch was prosperous, and potatoes became a money crop of no mean proportions. He found that he could mature his potatoes, sell them, and then grow a crop of cotton, making two crops instead of one on the same land. Of course he didn't have much time to loaf around and talk politics.

Within three years after this panic, the banks held more farmers' money on deposit than they ever had before. Merchants sold more goods for cash than they had previously sold on credit. In one small community there had been 2800 farm mortgages before the weevil came, and Mrs. Weevil cut down these encumbrances to 400.

Mrs. Weevil had never been to college except as a bottled specimen, yet she bestowed a liberal education upon that part of Texas, literally clubbing them into affluence.

It is said that the weevil caused more changes in the South than were brought about by the Civil War. Anyhow they ate the crop, ate the credit, and devoured a business system.

XI

WHIPPING THE WEEVIL

WHEN the world's most formidable enemy of agriculture attacks the world's most important crop, he's bound to start a fight, especially if that enemy attacks the property of fighting men. For a period of dazed bewilderment the South stood gasping at the suddenness, at the completeness of disaster; then began to look around for a weapon.

Planters like Colonel Darius Woodville were hardest hit because they grew long staple which requires more time to mature, and because of their negro labor which is less efficient. A white farmer will battle to save his home, while a negro tenant makes no persistent effort.

Wash Johnson might shut the door, call his dog and move, but Colonel Rye could not abandon the property. He was no quitter, yet thousands of intelligent Southerners feared that their country was forever gone as a producer of staple cotton. The delta climate is moist and favorable to propagation of the weevil. Thick forests often surround their fields and provide tree-bark for the pest to hibernate.

Something had to be done, and done right now. The same "spectacled professors" whom dirt farmers had pooh-poohed a few years ago, got busy at every experiment station in the South, developing varieties of cotton that would mature more quickly in advance of the weevil; and devising plans for intenser methods of culture.

When the female weevil punctures a "square" it shrivels and falls to the ground with the larvae inside; there the worm lies safe in the shade of the plant. If the stung square, however, drops in hot dust, the larvae dies, so the farmer now does a lot of plowing between his cotton rows, scratching up dirt and covering infested squares.

Wash Johnson growled mightily at the boss for putting so much extra work on him, but had to do it or he could draw no grub on Saturday night.

In early spring when weevils emerge from hibernation, punctured squares were picked up by hand and burned, which broke Wash Johnson's rest, and led him to suggest the scheme of making children help. Swarms of bare-legged black youngsters were sent to the fields, each carrying an empty tin can, and a can full of punctured squares was accepted as legal tender for a can full of candy at the commissary. By this simple plan, shirt-tailed pickaninnies destroyed millions of potential weevil.

Meantime chemists and inventors stepped into the picture, offering for sale all sorts of devices to apply poison. They had learned more about the pest, knew that Mrs. Weevil could not be killed by contact poisons, but must be reached in her food, or drink. Drink was easier, for when she rises at dawn Mrs.

FIGHTING THE BOLL WEEVIL WITH AIRPLANES AND CALCIUM ARSENATE

Weevil takes her morning sip from dew on the cotton leaf. Good! Man's defensive genius doses that sip of dew with calcium arsenate.

Desperate farmers tried everything, and Wash Johnson was forced to operate a squirt-gun by hand, or hitch his mules to a gimcrack that travelled on wheels. More trouble for Wash, more toil and sweat in the scorching sun, until white folks studied up another fool notion of killing weevil from the air. Of course the boss couldn't make Wash navigate a flying machine, so he lies in bed and listens while a white man does the work.

Saturday morning Wash had company in his cabin, Cousin Isom from Vicksburg who came out last night.

"What's dat?" At the first peep of day Isom sat up in bed and listened. "Wash, what's all dat fuss?"

" 'Tain't nothin'," Wash answered. "Roll over an' take another nap; den us'll go fishin'."

Dim grey daylight. A calm morning. Around Wash Johnson's cabin a moist fog hung listless above the cotton fields. Then suddenly through the dripping stillness, a roar came rushing upon them. Nearer, the tumult rattled their windows; it clamored against their cabin. A fury broke over the roof top. There was no chance to run, and Town Isom leaped out of bed, yelling, "Run, nigger, run. Cyclone's comin'!"

Wash Johnson never turned over, though his flimsy cabin trembled with the impact of crashing air. His door burst open and slammed. A crayon portrait fell from the wall—all in one swift moment, while Town Isom stood petrified. Then stillness again, silence again, as the roar passed on.

"What's dat?" Isom stuttered.

" 'Tain't nothin'," his country cousin grinned; "nothin' 'cept dese white folks is chasin' bugs wid deir flyin' machine."

"Flyin' machine? Lawd, it skacely missed yo' roof!"

"Sholy. Dey figgers on missin' a nigger shack by jest about one inch an' a half . . . Come back to bed."

Isom didn't go back to bed; he was considering, and inquired, "What reemarks did you make 'bout white folks chasin' bugs wid a flyin' machine?"

"Dat's what dey does. It's sineytific."

The visitor from town appeared incredulous, as though his country host were joshing him, and sneered, "Huh, white folks ought to have better sense. I don't believe dat."

"Don't b'leeve it? I'll prove dem facks. Dat feller's coming right back."

When the airplane flew back, along a parellel course, both negroes stood on Wash's gallery, watching the performance. Not higher than ten feet above the level cotton acres, the plane came skimming toward them. It almost seemed to graze the tops of growing plants, and left behind a trail of dense white powder, like an automobile on a dusty road.

"What's dat stuff, smoke?" Isom asked, and Wash Johnson chuckled as he answered, "Co'se not. Dat's salt, which dey sprinkles on his tail to make de weevils tame."

Back and forth the airplane sailed, throwing out its cloud of calcium arsenate, which a wind blast from the plane drove amongst the plants.

"Shucks," Isom scoffed. "Dey can't catch nary bug dat way."

"Hush yo' mouf, fool!" his country kinsman shut him up. "Never let nobody hear you laugh. When white folks is listenin', you praise dem airyplanes, praise 'em high. 'Cause ef dey warn't runnin' dat corntraption deirselves, de boss would make me git out and pizen dat cotton. Dis is de onliest time I ever heared a white man say, 'Step aside, nigger, an' lemme do dis work.' It's mighty seldom dat any nigger gits de chance to set in de shade an' watch a white man sweatin' in de sun."

Wash Johnson approves this scientific method of poisoning boll weevil from an airplane. Otherwise he must wrestle with a machine that travels along the ground at night, when dew has moistened the leaves and poison will adhere.

From a rocking-chair Wash could now sit and nod his satisfaction as the airplane whizzed above his crops, rose at the edge of his field, circled gracefully, and swooped down again. Criss-cross, in swaths three hundred feet wide, the plane distributed calcium arsenate by the new-fangled and supposedly scientific method of controlling a crop pest.

"Ain't dat nice? Jest look." The country negro patted his foot and hummed a tune. "Dat's what dese white folks calls sineytific."

"Sineytific, huh!" Isom corrected. "Ain't you never went to school? Den you ain't larnt nothin' 'cept to eat yo' lunch. Eddicated folks says si-un-tific."

"Either way, jest so dat white feller does my work."

Isom kept eying the plane and pondering, but couldn't catch on; finally he admitted, "I don't onderstand how dat thing operates. Co'se all dat fuss is bound to start plenty bugs, but how do he ketch 'em?"

"Dat's whar de sineytific part comes in."

"My ma warn't si-un-tific," the town negro laughed, "but ma could sholy start bugs, an' ketch 'em too. She had a big comb in her left hand, wid a little comb in her right hand—one starter an' one ketcher. She made me set down on de floor an' gripped my head 'twixt her kness. Den she grabbed 'em. I been noticin' dat feller mighty close, an' he ain't cotch nary one. Furthermo', he won't never ketch one, not ef he waits fer me to fly in dat thing an' help him."

"I flied—once," Wash grinned.

"You? How come? Crazy?"

"No. Cunnel went over to Tallooly, Loozianny, whar dey has dem flyin' machines, an' tuk me wid him. Den dem fellers 'ceived me. I was watchin' dat thing on de groun', whilst de white folks took pictures. My boss wanted his picter took, wid dat skullcap an' goggles on, settin' in de machine—jest fer biggity. Lot o' more white folks had deirn took. Den de photograph man say, 'Wash, like to have yo' beauty struck?' I said, 'Yas-suh; thankee, suh.' Co'se, I never 'spicioned 'em, jest climbed in whar dey tole me. Den two fellers stropped me tight, an' I couldn't git loose. Lordee! Befo' I knowed it dat white man done riz up.

"Dey aimed to cut shines in de sky, showin' off deir machine, an' needed a hundred an' fifty pounds o' nigger on de back seat to balance it. Dat nigger was me. Skeered? Ugh! Ugh! I sho gat dizzy when I seen de earth drappin' away onderneaf, an' felt my stummick drappin' wid it. Co'se I shet bofe eyes an' helt on like a chicken to de roost, ontil dat white man holler back, 'Look down, Wash! You is now flyin' over de cote house at Tallulah.' Look down? Not me. No, sir, I never did look down. It made me sick jest to cornsider lookin' down. Atter while I sorter opened one eye an' squinted up in de air; an' dar—way up yonder—dar was Talluly."

Wash Johnson is a pretty fair barometer of public opinion. To chase bugs with a flying machine? Huh! About 1922, when that crack-brained notion was first suggested, everybody laughed at it, even as you and I. The same people—you and I—had also jeered at the mosquito theory.

Years ago it was demonstrated that the female Stegomyia is the sole carrier of yellow fever, and we have no more epidemics.

Entomologists have also proven that boll weevil may be controlled by poison. But how apply it? If the fields are wet and boggy so that calcium arensate machines which run on the ground cannot be drawn through thickly growing plants, they use an airplane. To observe the maneuvers of a dusting plane it seems incredible that the poison can be so accurately distributed—at the very edge of a field, then shut off, and turned on again when the flier swoops back.

Flying in a duster plane gives a bigger thrill than scouting over boche lines with a French acrobat, and this writer has tried both. The war-flyer sails at lofty altitudes with no nearby object to mark his swiftness, consequently a passenger feels little sensation. A poison plane skims the earth at one hundred and twenty-five miles an hour, missing by a hair the roof of Wash Johnson's cabin, dodging like a rabbit amongst the trees, and assures a novice that he's not loafing.

Look out! There's an oak. We are headed straight for it. Another bat of an eye and the plane smashes. Hold your breath. There! No, the bird man climbs that tree, literally climbs it, one infinitesimal fraction of a second before the collision.

Half a yard this side he takes the upshoot. Your stomach takes the downshoot. Up we go. Up and over. Down again. We sail on a level, we straighten out, we run low, like a racer in the stretch, and turn on the poison.

No use warning this Borgia of the air that he'd better keep away from the woods. He must fly close; the worst infestation is there. For when Mrs. Weevil crawls out from winter quarters she wants food and patronizes the first lunch counter—a row of cotton nearest the timber. Besides, it's apt to be shadier there, and damper. Mrs. Weevil is a great drinker. She dotes on moisture, sucks it greedily. So the poisoner steers close to the brush, and shoots his calcium arsenate. The pilot has a trick of skidding sideways, holding the tail of his plane toward a thicket, so the powerful back draft blows poison where it's needed.

Air beginnings were jeered at by conservatives who objected that poverty-stricken farmers had already been bilked out of too much money by claptrap devices that did no good; that no farmer would be able to buy and fly an airplane. Visionaries made their original experiments in obsolete ships loaned by the War Department, but when the visionary succeeds, the conservative cashes in. Commercial corporations were formed to do the dusting as a business proposition at so much per acre for the season.

The charge by commercial companies, of approximately $5.50 an acre for dusting, may be materially reduced where a wider and consolidated acreage is served by a single dusting unit. Their principal cost is the overhead, which includes the maintenance of an organization for twelve months, when its actual labor is finished in a very few weeks—if limited to cotton. But other crops and other pests, at a different season, might easily be handled by the same outfit under the same overhead. Already the method is used for extensive peach orchards in Georgia.

Government experimenters claim that the cost of airplanes is not greater than the expense of dusting by hand, or by various ground contrivances.

Air poisoners have developed many facts and stumbled upon others. For example: by all former methods calcium arsenate was recommended to be applied at nights, when moisture on the foliage caused the powder to adhere. It was not supposed to stick if plants were dry. Then it began to be observed that even on dry days poison thrown from an airplane would cling to the leaf. Why? Did electricity cut a figure? Possibly. All plant life carries a negative charge. Dust in the hopper of a plane, subjected to a frenzied stirring, becomes highly positive. Each positive atom is repellent to its neighbor. So the molecules of dust when hurled out will separate, each to itself, giving a far greater diffusion. For that reason, less poison is required, and wasted, by an airplane than by a ground duster.

In course of dusting from the air, a dead tree may obstruct the field, or a high stump endanger the

fliers. These are cut away, incidentally removing
plague spots where millions of weevil hibernate, and
many a plantation is now tidied up shipshape.

Lenders of money began to be convinced, and
lands again became a bankable security. For a time
bankers at a distance maintained their hostile attitude that no credit should be advanced for such
frivolities as flying machines. But local financiers
now view it as a crop insurance—like a fire policy—
and lend greater sums if the farmer subscribes to a
dusting service. Hard-headed planters, after wit-
nessing the effects of poison spread gratis by Uncle
Sam's experimenters, began to make contracts with
commercial companies and pay for it. This is the
acid test of faith, and local banks, familiar with
results, willingly add that much extra to their lien
upon the crop. The larger loan, with insurance, is
regarded as a safer loan.

No one unfamiliar with the Cotton Belt is able
to conceive the panic of our farmers when Mrs.
Weevil began operating on their crops. Brave men,
whose axe and rifle had conquered this wilderness,
were ready to give up and surrender to a bug. They
quit cold, quit for a while, but couldn't stay licked.
Then came the psychological reaction of seeing
something done.

Everybody can see a flying machine—see it busy
—busy as a bumblebee in a tar bucket. Suppose the
pilot does nothing but buzz; he stimulates other
folks to buzz instead of sit.

From a combination of causes our cotton farmers have risen out of darkness and hold their faces in the light. The old fighting spirit has come back. They laugh again, but not at chasing Mrs. Weevil in a flying machine.

Since 1922, 90 per cent of our Cotton Belt has been infested by weevil, and pessimists predicted that Southern fields must be abandoned. Very well, let us compare the yield. Half a century ago, an acre of land east of the Mississippi River produced on an average 168 pounds of lint. Today, from that same acre, in spite of weevil, the farmer picks 219 pounds of lint, and gathered eighteen million bales in 1931. As James Whitcomb Riley used to say, " 'Tain't no man in the country more tickleder'n" Wash Johnson who can doze in the shade while a white feller runs his job.

XII

THE KING AND THE STAGE PLANK

THE Mississippi River is not merely a stream that flows through lands. It is a personality, vague, mysterious, malicious; or prodigal in its bounties. From prehistoric yesterdays our river remains the same through long lone stretches of solitude. Modern progress has never tamed the wildness of its shores because every season its waters cover the land outside the levees where man can erect no permanent work.

Hidden behind huge embankments are intensively cultivated farms. Tractors plow the cotton fields, but you cannot see them from the river. Railroads and concrete highways run through level miles and busses carry children to consolidated schools. Yet not even a church spire is visible from the passing boat, so a voyager in 1937 sees exactly what DeSoto saw, tawny sandbars, jungles of willow and cottonwood, and caving banks that belong to the river, will always belong to the river.

In its march from the Atlantic to the Pacific, civilization skipped over this jagged strip of land between the levee and low water edge, leaving there forever the republic's last frontier, unclaimed and irreclaimable.

Towards the end of the eighteenth century canoes began to paddle southward carrying pelts for sale at New Orleans in defiance of the Spanish king who had ordered Kentuckians to keep off his river. *His* river? No sirree, as they contended the Mississippi belongs to Kentucky, and any foreigner who tries to block it had better hunt a hole.

Settlers beyond the Alleghanies felt rabidly about their river, Kentucky's only outlet to the sea, her sole channel of communication with the world. Already they launched their awkward crafts, and followed in the wake of adventurous canoes. By flatboat and "broadhorn" muscular arms propelled their produce to the den of the Spanish don. This represented the first commercial use of our river by white men who boasted themselves half alligator, half horse, forerunners of a prodigious traffic.

As population poured into the Ohio country, farmers sent down the river wheat and potatoes, corn and hogs in unwieldy scows, square at both ends, with high gunwales and three stout tree forks on either side that served as row locks for enormous paddle sweeps. Brawny frontiersmen toiled at the sweeps wearing nondescript garb, part-Indian, part-white, with tomahawk and rifle to fight off river pirates until they reached the Crescent City.

Flatboat trade grew so marvelously that New Orleans leaped at once to second place in the rank of American ports, passing Baltimore, Philadelphia and Boston. By 1820 more than half the exports of this nation threatened to leave America through the Gulf of Mexico.

New fields along the river were being cleared for cotton when, in 1811, Nicholas Roosevelt, Fulton, and Livingston attempted to navigate western rivers with their steamboat, the *Orleans*. Fulton's *Clermont* was not the first steamboat, but the eleventh, ten others having preceded her in more or less successful operation.

Fulton constructed the *Orleans* on a deep sea model, suitable for the tidewater Hudson but unfit to run the sandbars and shallows of the Mississippi. Downstream she moved most gallantly at the unbelievable speed of fourteen days from Pittsburgh to New Orleans. Then Pittsburgh never saw that boat again, for her feeble engines could not get back upstream.

Five years later, Captain Henry M. Shreve perfected Fulton's idea, just as Fulton had improved the designs of Blasco de Garay's side-wheeler built at Barcelona in 1543.

Shreve, a hard-headed river rat, had a notion that to skim over shallows his craft must be able, in pilot parlance, to "float on a heavy dew and turn around on a dime." Marine engineers jibed at him, yet he persisted in constructing a "top-heavy tug" on a keelboat hull. His machinery, which weighed onetwentieth of Fulton's, he placed on deck instead of below it, and succeeded so triumphantly that all Mississippi packets have since followed his design.

Fifty such steamers were launched in 1829, and by the close of 1832, ninety thousand persons were gaining their livelihood in the business of navigation.

In moving such a vast and sudden business there could be little system. Boats departed whenever they could. Hundreds of cotton bales lay tiered upon the banks while passengers camped beside the river and waited. Maybe the steamer might come tomorrow. Gradually the haphazard packets settled down to regular timetables, and a merchant might count upon the day, almost upon the hour, when his goods would arrive.

Valley life centered around the packets, and King Cotton crossed their stageplanks with thousands of his bales. The steamer was more than a vehicle of transportation, for the captain served his friends as errand boy, as purchasing agent, as go-between, and maintained a staff at New Orleans to perform duties that were beyond the scope of a common carrier for hire. If Colonel Woodville needed a gin belt, Captain Ramsey was glad to buy it, or maybe he'd stop to deliver one small bottle of angostura bitters so that Colonel Rye could have his cocktail.

On her up-trip the packet might nose into a perilous landing and lie there two hours, while her captain, wearing a long-tailed coat, high hat, frilly shirt, his diamond studs linked together by golden chains —while the splendid captain went ashore bearing a bouquet for a little sick girl.

These services were rendered partly from a spirit

of neighborliness, and in part with the object of making patrons for the boat. Many a planter let packet after packet go by and held a hundred bales for his favorite.

The earnings of a popular boat were enormous. Receipts had to be large for the average life of a steamer was about five years. Snags sunk them, fires and explosions and sandbars. Within a brief period the packet must repay its cost, say $200,000, and show a profit.

Floating palaces of white and gold lent romance to the river. Youngsters made love on the guards, and danced in cabins that glittered with prismatic chandeliers. Staggering stakes were wagered in poker games. At mealtime the white-jacketed waiter rang his bell for a dinner epicures could find no fault with. In his department the steward was supreme, and no master questioned a single dollar that he spent.

Passengers gathered at big tables in the cabin, tables that gleamed with glass and silver. Vases of brilliant flowers. Baskets piled high with tropical fruits. Appetizers. Soups, meats, chickens, turkeys, fish, oysters, shrimp, crabs. Venison, bear meat, acres of assorted pies and endless flavors of ice cream. It seemed impossible for boats to serve such a profusion of luxuries at the price of a cabin fare.

Whenever the *White Cloud* approached Woodville Plantation, every woman on the property, unless she had both legs broke, would swarm at the landing to see her tie up and make goo-goo eyes at the crew. Airily as a swan the packet wafted herself inshore to pick up Colonel Woodville's cotton. The mate rushed out his gang of forty rousters, forty negroes trotting in single file, singing and "coonjining" across the stageplank.

The "coonjine" seems an institution peculiar to our river, and suggests what it is, a rhythmic melody, keeping time, time, time to the patter of bare feet that strike the stageplank. The plank sways and swings in unison with moving bodies, this way, that way, up, down, as rousters roll aboard the heavy bales.

"See dat ooman? On de sack pile?" a coonjiner bursts out extemporaneously,

> "She's a grinnin'. She's a smilin',
> Big white teeth at me.
> I got money—come here, honey—"

The song flows on and on, its words change, but the melody is never broken.

The *White Cloud* was loaded. Negroes crowded to the banks and cheered. The Captain lifted his hat to Colonel Rye, and the Colonel saluted him in return. The pilot blew a melodious whistle. Bells jangled in the engine room. Rousters cast loose their lines and scrambled aboard. The stageplank swings in. Captain Ramsey poses on the hurricane deck beside a big brass bell. Paddle wheels revolve.

THE MISSISSIPPI RIVER IS STILL A GREAT ARTERY OF COTTON TRANSPORTATION

Sunlight sparkles upon her gilded fretwork as the *White Cloud* backs out with bands playing and every flag aflutter.

The packets carried Colonel Woodville's cotton and monopolized river traffic until Federal gunboats swept them away in the sixties. After the restoration of peace they came back with a bang. Ship yards along the Ohio turned them out by the hundreds and Father Mississippi glittered again for a brilliant decade of renaissance.

The depression of 1873 was followed by a frenzied era of railroad construction in the eighties, and locomotives snorted along both banks of the Mississippi snatching freight from startled packets. By the turn of the century rail competition had driven out our steamboats. All were gone, the *Lee*, the *Natchez*, the gorgeous *Grand Republic*, and simply to mention their names within hearing of a river-born lad is like calling the role of heroes.

Scarcely a packet plied the lower river until 1917 when America entered the World War and rail facilities broke down under a terrific strain. Thousands of box cars congested in freight yards and could not be moved. To supplement transportation and relieve a rail paralysis, all sorts of water equipment was commandeered and barge line service established under control of the War Department. After the armistice this service has been continued, as a common carrier for hire. In addition to Federal barges, several private lines are now in operation. It is said that Uncle Sam means to give the river another chance, and if his venture be profitable, he plans to sell out and let private enterprise handle the traffic.

XIII

CREVASSES

MISSISSIPPI RIVER levees, and a wheelbarrow contraption invented by Leonardo da Vinci, taught wild Irishmen to stand on their hind legs and walk like men.

The Creole planter in lower Louisiana piled up his first flimsy barricade with slaves and shovels, until parishes united in levee construction as a public work, when regiments of shaggy Irish began to trundle their barrows full of dirt. They used plank runways, dumping along the growing ridge, and being paid by the piece, at so much per cubic yard, they'd sneak in an empty barrel or box and cover it over—to measure in their yardage. Crawfish bored holes in the embankments which broke and furnished another job, so to this day a crawfish is known as "The Irishman's Friend."

As modern methods developed, a slip scraper and single mule, usually driven by a plantation negro, supplanted the Irishman's barrow; then a double scraper and two mules, that built more solid levees because the trampling of mules would pack the soft earth. For colossal projects in the past few years, machines of unthinkable power are employed, tractors, "revolving turrets" and "drag lines" whose ponderous "shovels" carry more material at one load in one minute than an Irishman's barrow might handle in a week.

All levees, however, could not at once be raised to "commission grade and standard" by which is meant the specifications of U. S. Engineers when Uncle Sam stepped into the picture. No standard embankment ever broke, weaker lower defenses always being first to give way.

"Come here, Gordon." Colonel Rye beckoned his manager into the office and whispered, "Don't start a panic, but send out half a dozen reliable tenants and round up all our stock. Then drive them to the hills."

"Yes, sir," the manager answered. "I'm afraid the levee's going out."

"Looks that way. Water's brimming over its top, with two more feet coming down from Cairo."

"How about the women and children?" Gordon asked. "Hadn't I better make them get ready, and if a break happens, rush everybody to the Indian mound?"

"No use, yet," the veteran planter shook his head. "You know how bull-headed our negroes are about deserting their cabins. Won't believe an overflow's coming until it gets up to their necks."

Delta people usually refused to believe that a crevasse might occur, and persisted in fighting to the last, thus often holding their levees.

"Don't get excited, boy." Colonel Woodville patted Gordon on the shoulder and smiled through a silver-white mustache. "We've floundered through so much water that I've got web-footed. Save our stock and I'll try to hold the levee."

Men of sense realized that such embankments couldn't stand against a flood that would overtop them by three feet, so every planter fought to maintain his own defense, until the break and the destruction occurred at some other point.

When Colonel Woodville reached the river front and glanced at the levee, he felt a moment's restoration of confidence. From the land side these gigantic fortifications seemed impregnable, a towering titanic rampart that guarded the frontier of the world. He couldn't see the river, but knew that beyond the levees' crown, water was piling up, water, water, water, higher than any dyke could stand against.

Hundreds of men, white and black, were frantically filling sacks with dirt, while other hundreds marched up the slope in single file bearing sacks upon their shoulders to where they'd be laid in place. Along the ridge, north and south as far as he could see, still other thousands toiled; and unseen thousands stretched beyond his range of vision.

The planter leaped from his car and ran zigzag up the slope, noting that two additional tiers of sacks had been laid since he went home half an hour ago. This he hoped might give them breathing time, but the river was mounting faster than bags could be laid.

The yellow monster attacked with incredible force, and human midgets were trying to beat him back. Hopeless. Hopeless.

The crown of Ruthven levee was less than six feet wide because the engineers had not yet got around and strengthened it. Along its outer edge, next to the devouring river, a temporary barricade of planks extended for miles to protect the loose dirt against wave wash. Half a gale blew, and ravenous waters licked at the soft earth that melted and fell away. White men and negroes stood waist deep in the waves, nailing on planks. With haggard eyes they gazed at Colonel Woodville, telling their story of defeat.

"Here, boy," the boss reached down and gave a hand to one of his negroes, pulling him from the water, "go home and rest. You're worn out. Give me that hammer."

Colonel Rye had just started to take the tenant's place and drive nails, when a sudden cry burst out, "Help! Quick! Help!"

"Look dere!" a black man screamed, and turned grey with terror as he pointed at the crest. "Look! Look!"

The saturated levee was settling down like mush, slipping, sliding, caving into the river. A huge crack appeared; tons of dirt sloughed off to melt and wash away. "Run, men, run," Colonel Rye shouted.

Tenants scurried like rabbits, splashed through seepage water at the base of the levee and were gone. Colonel Woodville stood another moment and saw the last thin remnant as it broke. A sudden collapse, the earthen ridge sank gently, quietly. A gap showed at the top, a gap that filled with frothy bubbly water, as though myriads of triumphant demons were rushing through a breach in the conquered fortress. The planter stood fascinated by its sheer magnificence and watched a victorious mass that thundered through with a roar. Then he too ran down the slope.

On the lower level panicky autos were starting. They must beat the water to the highway; in two minutes more their plantation road would go out. Negroes scrambled on mules and raced off; others trusted to their legs.

When Colonel Woodville in his car reached the gravelled road, water was already skimming over it. A flying negro on a mule waved his hand and shouted, "Don't go dat way, Cunnel. Dis road's cut off at de bayou."

Soon the crevasse had widened until twice the downpour of Niagara swept across Ruthven. Logs went swirling past, and struggling animals. Waters rioted among the forest, carrying negro cabins to smash against trees.

After gushing out from the jaws of the crevasse, the first mad torrent spread out and diffused itself across the flatlands, where thousands of isolated families lived, white farmers and black farmers, women, children, cows, mules, all helpless in the path of destruction which would end only at the bluffs of Vicksburg. Farmers in the back country had a little time to prepare, possibly a few hours. Small boats came, skiffs, dugouts, batteaux, rafts, every imaginable thing that would float, and bore them to safety. Day and night the rescuers searched every thicket, every cabin, telephone poles, trees, so that not one single person was overlooked.

Nearer the front, by wading, swimming or using boats, farmers and most of their livestock were concentrated upon unbroken levees. There was nowhere else to go, for with a turbulent Mississippi on one side and crevasse rapids on the other, levees offered the only solid land.

For days this submerged area was a nightmare of hysteria, the saving of human life, picking up of cattle, then it settled down into a watery solitude from which all living creatures had departed. Only the vultures remained, circling around in empty skies and feeding on carcases.

Steamboats nosed up to the levees bringing barges on which refugees were loaded thick as they could stand, and carried to the Gibraltar hills at Vicksburg.

The population of that town doubled overnight by the addition of twenty-five thousand wet, hungry and impoverished cotton farmers.

The same catastrophe happened all over Southern

Louisiana where the magnitude of disaster appalled our nation. The Red Cross came, the U. S. Army, senators, representatives, and cabinet ministers to see for themselves, to witness damages far greater than would be the cost of prevention for all time.

XIV

THE KING AND HIS REBELLIOUS RIVER

BEFORE modern levees were built so high and strong, an overflow didn't always cause much destruction. Having no stout embankments to burst through, the waters rose gradually and spread over level cotton lands, with plenty of space to flatten out. So they made no swirling currents that picked up negro cabins and tossed them about like eggshells. Slowly the floods receded and, as compensation for any damage, left behind them a deposit of fertilizing silt which grew astounding crops.

Old Hamp, the veteran bear hunter, had belonged to Colonel Damascus Woodville before the Civil War, and still made headquarters at Ruthven where he and Colonel Rye were close friends. The Colonel let him keep his cabin, and Hamp occasionally came back to it. Then the two old cronies would sit on the front porch and reminisce, the planter in a rocking chair while Hamp squatted on the top step and leaned against the broad white column.

"Cunnel," the tall brown negro remarked, " 'pears to me dere's a heap mo' water nowadays dan what yo' pa used to git."

"No, we don't get any more water, but it rushes down on us all at once, because forests have been

126

cut away at the north and fields cleared. Instead of seeping through grass and woods, it runs off now like rain from a roof."

"Is dat de way of it? Anyway in 1882 de *Rosa May* got sucked through a crevasse at de same place where yo' levee busted las' spring, an' went whirlin' 'cross dat field where yo' plows is workin' at. Hit dat sycamore. Cunnel, I come down from Memphis on dat trip o' de *Rosa May,* an' since den I ain't been no han' to prank wid ole Miss'ip when she's fixin' to bust loose."

"You were on that boat? When she got wrecked?"

"Sho was," came the prompt response. "I'd been huntin' in Arkansas but de whole country went under water an' I was tryin' to git home.

"Anyhow I kotched de *Rosa May* at Memphis. Whalin' big boat, stout as a flock o' bulls. It was her first trip down de river an' she had one o' dese smart-aleck cap'ns. De pilot steered close inshore so her passengers could see de big water. Huh! I jest couldn't keep my mouf shut. Here we come, bulgin' downstream, puffin' an' blowin', actin' biggety. So I sidles up alongside de cap'n an' says, 'Dat water's powerful deceivin'. Us better steer away from dem crevasses.' "

" 'Where's yo' pilot license?' de cap'n asked me. *'I'm* runnin' dis boat.'

"Sho nuff, Cunnel, him an' de pilot was runnin' it. Atter while dey run her smack jam in a crevasse. De *Rosa May* quivered, den went slidin' 'long, same as if she was slippin' down hill. Lordee, how dem bells jangled an' dem firemen throwed wood in de furnace. Passengers run ev'y which way. De pilot spins round an' round on his wheel, whilst de *Rosa May* backed and splashed and kicked, but 'twarn't no use. Ole Miss had done reached up an' grabbed her. Atter a turrible scufflin' she straightened out an' tuk a shoot through de crevasse. 'Don't jump! Don't jump!' Cap'n rushed around like a crazy man, beggin' his passengers to stay on de boat. Now we went through dat cravasse, crashin' amongst dem willers. Wimmens was screamin', an' 'peared like nobody knowed what to do.

"Curyus, ain't it, Cunnel," old Hamp chuckled, "de things which a man cornsiders in dem times. All de way from Memphis I'd been wonderin' how I was goin' to git home. 'Twarn't nary place to land on neither side de river. Ef a levee warn't already broke, white men wid shotguns was guardin' it, warnin' us to keep off. 'Peared like I'd go plum to Vicksburg befo' de *Rosa May* could drap a stage-plank. Shucks!

"All of a sudden us went tearin' through a new crevasse an' headed fer dis plantation. So I grins to myself an' say, 'Ef I does git spilt, I'll git spilt at home.'

"Next thing I cornsidered was a lady which was huddlin' two little boys an' awful skeered. I goes up to her wid my hat in my han' an' says, ' 'Scuse me, ma'am, lemme have dese chillun an' I'll git 'em out, no matter ef dis boat do sink.'

"Some white folks is got sense. Dat lady tuk one squint at me an' say, 'I'll trust you wid my sons.' Dat was all.

"I cut me a piece o' rope an' tied dem youngsters' wrists together, 'bout two yards apart, so dey couldn't git loose from me. Ef us was flung in de water I could drag 'em ontil I kotch a limb.

"Bless yo' soul, Cunnel, it didn't take no time fer de *Rosa May* to reach dis plantation, tearin' through briar patches an' bumpin' 'mongst de woods. Den us struck de open field, dat very field out yonder, an' hit de sycamore. 'Co'se, de swiftest current run through yo' slough, an' I figgered it would throw us ag'inst de ridge at Bullhorn. So I says, 'Cap'n, we'se 'proachin' some high ground. Gimme a line an' I'll pass it round a tree. Maybe you kin hold her.'

"Twarn't no trick, Cunnel. I knowed where de shallers was, an' when dem roustabouts seen me jump wid a line in water less'n knee-deep, dey follered wid mo' lines. Huh! Dem passengers helt deir breff whilst dem lines drawed tight. Den de *Rosa May* stopped and de passengers could be took off in skiffs.

"After de water went down it sho did look comercal to see a steamboat perched on Bullhorn Ridge twenty miles from de river. But de white man what owned her didn't see nothin' funny, an' never said nothin' funny neither. Lord, Lord, Cunnel, when I tuk him dere to look at his boat, dat white man cussed a blue streak, cussed de pilot, cussed de cap'n, called 'em ev'ything except a child o' God. Den he kinder snickered an' 'spressed hisself, 'Good-by, *Rosa May.* Dere you lays; dere you stays.'

"For de longest kind o' time whenever dese plantation hands needed a cabin door, or a lock or most anything, dey tuk it from de wreck, ontil de *Rosa May* was ontirely toted off."

"Hamp," the planter asked, "that was in 1882, you say? The river didn't actually rise as high that year as it does now."

" 'Twarn't de highness of it, Cunnel, what caused so much worriment, but de slowness of runnin' off. Dat's de year yo' grampa made his big-toe crop.

"Yas, suh," Hamp leaned back against his post and got a fresh start. "Yo' grampa sho was pestered. Dat fust rampage o' water lodged de *Rosa May* on Bullhorn; den de overflow went down five or six feet an' stopped runnin' off. Fell a little mo', got jest about shoe-top deep all over dis plantation an' quit fallin'. Dere it reemained an' reemained. By dat time in de year cotton ought to be knee-high, but it warn't even planted.

"Ev'y mornin' yo' grampa would come out on dis gallery an' look at his fields, den ramble back in de house. Wuss an' wuss. Gittin' later an' later.

"Somethin' was bleeged to be did, an' yo' grampa was a powerful shifty man. One day I sees him trompin' up an' down dis gallery, ponderin' an' ponderin'; den he grabbed de bannisters an' yelled, 'Hamp! Hamp!'

" 'Hamp,' he say, 'I'm fixin' to plant my land anyhow. Got a-plenty seed an' de tenants is idle.'

"An', Cunnel, what yo' grampa aimed to do sounded reasonable. Warm water lay over de fields in a skim; de land was soft an' rich as cream. Ef he could git dem seed in de ground dey sho would grow. His main trouble was wid de niggers.

" 'Send fer Judy Mullin, to start 'em,' says I.

" 'Fine,' say ole Marster.

" 'An' git Alec wid his drum,' says I.

" 'The very thing,' says ole Marster; 'wid Jonas and his toot horn. We'll set dem niggers whoopin' an' plant our seed.'

"Cunnel, you ain't fergot Judy Mullin. She was a young gal den, an' de likeliest wench on dis property. An' Judy had a way about her. Done things like she wanted an' never waited fer nobody else to set de style. No harm in what Judy done, an' she had de men traipsin' atter her. 'Co'se dat injuced other young gals to tread in Judy's footsteps.

"Dat night me an' ole Marster trained Judy in how she was to act. Lordee, Cunnel, it would make yo' heart glad to see dat gal. Warn't skeered o' nothin'.

"So yo' grampa sends out word for his tenants to 'semble nex' mornin'. Dis yard had done got dry. Ev'y las' one of 'em come.

"Dat horn an' drum kept 'em grinnin', whilst old

Marster 'splained dat a few draps o' water couldn't bluff his tenants and cut off deir rations. Dey was goin' to make a crop in spite o' de whole Miss'ip River. Den he tole 'em how he aimed to plant, by wadin' over de fields an' trompin' in seed wid deir big toe.

"Huh! All dem niggers commenced glancin' at one annuder kinder sheepish an' helt back ontil Judy sot down on dese steps an' shucked her shoes, den pulled off her stockings, den her top skirt, an' commenced rollin' up her petticoat. At de same time yo' grampa, wid fo' managers an' two clerks in de sto', kicked off deir shoes and rolled up deir breeches fer wadin'.

"Den ole Marster stood up an' specify dat he aimed to git in de water his own self. De drums beat an' horns tooted.

"Fer a minit dem udder gals kinder hesitated to git barelegged. Dat's when Judy commenced to sing: 'One mo' river, one mo' river to cross. One mo' river, one mo' river to cross,'

an' sot 'em all to shoutin'. In less'n a minit de whole caboodle was lined up, fixed fer wadin', a man an' a gal, a man an' a gal. Yo' grampa spaced 'em far apart to tech hands an' plant dem cotton rows at even distance. 'Forward march!' say ole Marster, an' dey started off like skummishers in de war, drappin' seed, three at ev'y step, an' trompin' 'em in.

" 'Co'se ole Marster waded like de rest of 'em

across dis fust big field. An', Lordee, what a shout went up from all dem niggers when old Marster pitched forward on his face an' come up black as a nigger hisself from de mud. I cornsiders dat ole Marster done dat on purpose."

"And how did the cotton grow?"

"Grow? Fine ain't no name fer de way dat cotton sprouted. 'Peared like his plantin' squad would skarcely wade to de far side of a field befo' de cotton behind 'em done sprung up.

"Huh!" Hamp came to the end of his talkativeness. "I jest been settin' here watchin' yo' plows, an' studyin' 'bout de *Rosa May,* wid Judy an' her big-toe crop. Sometimes white folks squawks an' hollers 'bout the way things is goin', an' fergits de pesterments we used to have. But, Lord, Lord, on dis plantation, ole Marster always mixed his fun wid our troubles."

2

Since the dawn of time farmers have fought against water for possession of fertile bottoms. These debatable lands in our Mississippi Valley represent the finest of long staple cotton, and sugar fields of Southern Louisiana for whose defense the age-old struggle has gone on more than two centuries, and now we hope is successfully ended by a double line of dirt embankment five hundred miles longer than the great Wall of China and twenty-five times as thick.

Ages ago the Upper Mississippi, the Missouri and

the Ohio Rivers had never met, but emptied by separate mouths into an arm of the sea that extended inland from the Gulf of Mexico to cover the southern half of what is now the State of Illinois.

All three rivers brought down deposits of mud, building steadily before them until they came together at the site of Cairo, Illinois. Their united waters swept on, bringing dirt, dirt, dirt through all the patient eons, filling, filling, filling between irregular bluffs on either side their present bed. Southward the Mississippi flowed, dropping its burden of dirt into the narrow estuary and building up the alluvial country. Farther southward it reached the Yazoo Basin, a huge settling pool into which the river poured its richest silt. Century after century Father Mississippi dumped fertilizer into the Yazoo Basin, depositing treasure as if in a savings bank to be drawn upon by future generations. It was a tedious process filling this enormous delta, as big as Delaware added to Connecticut, half the arable area of modern Egypt.

Slowly the bottom rose, driving back the Yazoo River to its hills. "Let there be land." And there was land, but not a land to brag about, nothing but mush, too thick for a fish to swim in and too thin for a mosquito to stand upon.

The land grew higher, higher. Successive overflows added layer after layer of top soil until definite ridges showed themselves along the streams where the first and heaviest deposit was dropped. At the mouth of the Mississippi this same process still goes on, still extends year by year into the Gulf of Mexico.

A dapper little Frenchman who died two centuries ago started all this levee building, Le Blond de la Tour. From his name we may imagine him with a curly wig, jewelled snuffbox, and silver buckles on his shoes. He served as a Royal Engineer officer for King Louis, who graciously stuck him down in knee-deep slush at New Orleans. Every spring the few dozen exiles who waded around in that infant city were drowned out by a wet, cold river, and made such bedraggled pleas that something had to be done. So de la Tour commandeered a squad of barefoot blacks and threw up what he called a "levee" just one mile long and waist high. A joke of a levee, yet a most excellent joke, because it did bar out the floods. When Father Mississippi found himself kissed off along the New Orleans front, he merely sniffed a time or two at their childish barricade, and didn't take the trouble to break it. He could go somewhere else, go meandering into swamps and bayous at the rear. De la Tour's ridge might still be making New Orleans safe for creole gumbo if other embankments had not been raised by copycats who planted indigo on adjacent lands. Farmers built haphazard ridges, every fellow intent upon shunting water off his own crop.

Teamwork soon became desirable, so l'Avocat Dieudonne linked his private line to that of Chevalier de Montargis. Neighbor joined neighbor. Communities made common cause against a common enemy. Parish allied itself with parish, and imposed levee taxes. States helped, until as decades went by, fighting the river became a consolidated affair in Louisiana, Mississippi and Arkansas.

Try to imagine the vast extent of our Mississippi watershed, from the Appalachians to the Rockies. Pour a bucket of water on the ground in Southwestern New York, another bucket at Helena, Montana, and they combine to deluge the alluvial lands— water spouts in Wyoming, chunk floaters in Pennsylvania, melting snows in lower Canada, all join forces to come roaring down our valley.

Our entire river population swarms to the levee, working like ants, filling sacks with dirt and raising their flimsy barricade to keep off the flood. Every foot of levee was patrolled every minute. By night thousands of lanterns swung low against the ground to seek out the slightest weakness and watch every trickle of seepage. No people on earth ever fought harder for two centuries, paying all the costs of levee building, and standing all the loss of flood destruction.

Levee construction was, of course, abandoned during the Civil War. Federal troops cut our dykes, and not until 1869 was any serious effort made to rebuild by local taxation. During that period of heartbreak here's a record of results and gradual progress.

Inundations of 1882 burst through at 284 crevasses

to sweep away 56 miles of levee; in 1883 we had 224 crevasses with 34 miles of destroyed banks. By 1903 crevasses were reduced to seven, with 2.25 miles of embankments washed away.

As the river tore down their fortifications, cotton farmers with undismayed courage piled them up again, until overflows became fewer and farther apart in point of time. Crevasses in 1912 and 1913, however, jolted them again, then the unprecedented calamity of 1927.

As Oliver Cromwell once said, "Things have to get much worse before they get any better." Things did get so much worse that they began to get better, because the nation was finally aroused. Heretofore Uncle Sam had been helping local levee boards so partially and grudgingly that we must go back a bit to comprehend his frame of mind.

Valley dwellers had complained and complained of Father Mississippi's propensity to carry off their crops, but Uncle Sam insisted it was none of his business how badly the river cut up, provided it didn't leave a lot of sandbars lying around loose to interfere with navigation. Uncle had always contended that his job under the constitution is to keep open a gangway for steamboats, so that citizens may travel and U. S. mails go through. Therefore every time the river left a snag sticking up, or dumped a chunk of mud about the size of Connecticut, Uncle trailed along behind to fix that part of it. But on pay day when Uncle dug into his jeans and appropriated a dollar, he never failed to remind us: "Listen, boys, this money is for improvement of navigation. I won't spend a counterfeit nickel for protection of land."

Being uncommonly pig-headed he stuck to his original proposition and claimed jurisdiction only of the channel. Beyond the usual track of navigation, valley dwellers must shift for themselves; and though Uncle felt sorry, nevertheless if the river took a notion to slosh over its banks and devour miles of plantations or eliminate a few towns from the map, incidentally drowning a flock of hayseeds who couldn't swim, why, that was their lookout.

As years rolled on more and more people came to live in our valley, floods grew worse and worse until Uncle changed his mind a little and began to help us build levees. He excused himself by saying that embankments contracted the stream and made it scour a deeper channel for steamboats to carry mail, all the time winking his left eye if a levee happened to hold off water from a few acres of cotton. Gradually it became an established firm, this partnership of "Uncle and States" in preventing overflows. Before that, however, in spite of our pleading he had attended strictly to the post-roads clause and let Southern drys keep dry if they could.

In April 1927 the whole Mississippi Valley went wet, wet with a wallop—prohibitionists, bootleggers, everybody.

Many a springtime when the river did not feel

particularly peppy, it traveled sluggishly between levees, gnawing here and biting yonder for men to repair when its sullenness subsided. Those years the water did little harm, but in the early summer of 1927 the river gathered in overwhelming force.

Remember that an enormous dirt trough, brimful of water, ran through the middle of this continent. On either side lay farms and towns and homes, ten to twenty feet lower than the rim of the trough. Water from thirty-one states and part of Canada came raging down the valley, wave upon wave and crest upon crest, until our levees collapsed.

For three months unleashed floods submerged us, destroying more than $250,000,000 in property.

A manful howl uprose. Everybody hollered. The North chorused, the West chimed in. Brave men and women throughout the world felt a sympathy for other brave men and women who struggled so courageously to defend themselves. Help poured upon us like an avalanche, generous help that warms the heart—not the money, but the kindness of it. Then we caught our breath, held meetings and sent more delegations to confer with Uncle Sam.

The disaster made a different dent in his head. American lives were lost and American homes were wrecked on American soil, so Uncle Samuel broadened his interpretation of the post-roads clause. At first, like a bathing beauty, he had only dallied flirtatiously around the river's edge, careful not to go deeper than post-roads. Now he dived in, body and breeches, and started a war to end wars. Congress also got riled and passed a law with teeth in it, 325,-000,000 teeth.

That's how Uncle got into this job. Once being in it, neck deep, he proposes that the river channel shall carry every drop of water it can safely pass on to the Gulf, and to divert the surplus by such outlets as Nature has indicated.

A statement of what is known as "The Adopted Plan" sounds extremely simple, but working out details involved an incredible amount of labor by the foremost engineers of the world. If there be competent engineers on earth, we have them in America. Of the best, many go into the Army; and the pick of Army engineers have been assigned to this task. Associated with them are dozens of civilians especially trained by a lifetime of fighting high water—able, earnest, honest men. They have no local interests to serve, no local bosses to obey, and not a dime's worth of pecuniary profit to expect.

From a national viewpoint, representing the people of the entire valley, they first considered the plan as a whole, balanced the unavoidable disadvantages of certain communities against the greatest good of the greatest number.

Uncle Sam never does things half way. After abandoning his former attitude that he wouldn't spend a counterfeit nickel for protection of property, he now instructs his agents by special act of Congress that "all diversion works and outlets shall be built in a manner and of a character that will fully and amply protect adjacent lands." Before he gets through, Uncle is determined not only to render comparatively harmless such inundations as we have previously experienced, but even to guard against the maximum flood now predicted as possible.

In planning a campagin no cautious general neglects to inform himself of the enemy's force, so Uncle Sam has been investigating to discover what is the biggest army of water that the Mississippi can mobilize. This is not altogether guesswork. We have our own accurate records for upwards of forty years, showing the extent of rainfall and run-off. Beyond that point American experts have consulted European statistics under similar conditions, for more than two centuries. From this mass of data our specialists base their predictions of a superflood.

Superflood? What does that mean? It signifies the largest possible deluge that every tributary river, creek and rivulet can pour simultaneously into the Mississippi. Simultaneously. If we have cloudbursts in Montana; a colossal Ohio River; if Oklahoma and Texas are afloat; if the Missouri, Cumberland, Tennessee, Arkansas and Red all go raving mad so as to reach the Mississippi at once. Emphasize "at once." To produce a superflood, mountains of water cannot follow mountains of water— not *follow*. Every drop must pile up in the same place at the same time.

The Upper Mississippi, Missouri, Arkansas,

White, and Red may do whatever they darn please, and the vast channel of the Mississippi will handle it without spilling a gallon, provided some of the easterly rivers, Ohio, Cumberland, Tennessee, keep comparatively quiet. No superflood will occur except by a sinister combination of every factor.

A superflood is, therefore, the remotely possible but improbable theoretical maximum which may happen about once in every two hundred years. However, as we hope that America will still be doing business at the same old stand in 2136 A.D., Uncle Sam looks far ahead to save his posterity from being drowned.

Before trying to realize any scheme for harnessing of the Mississippi, we must first know why he so persistently breaks loose. The reason goes back to the age of mastodons and dinosaurs. Originally this river had but one low-water channel until it reached the flat lands; there, when great floods came, it overspread an area fifty miles wide. All that country is the natural high-water bed of the Mississippi which man has taken by artificial barricades and which man must in part restore. Unless we provide safety valves at points of our own choosing, then the river bursts out at far more destructive points.

The plain fact is that in the past half century Father Mississippi has been robbed of so much land that insufficient room is left for his superfloods to pass. Man has planted the river's ancient playground with cotton, corn and cane. Here man has built homes, school-houses, churches; reclaimed swamps are criss-crossed by modern highways. Locomotives whistle where old Bruin used to growl, and moccasins swam unmolested. But never forget that American sweat and blood wrested this jungle from barbarism and established a civilization which we refuse to surrender.

A stubborn race like ours hates to retreat from territory it has fought for and conquered, though many of us admit that we have plundered too much space from the river. There must be a compromise between man and the Mississippi. We must give back a little to save the balance, just as that wise old beaver bit off his tail to save his hide.

Before we revised our notions, river folks pinned their faith to levees only, building ridges high enough and strong enough to curb the Mississippi within definite bounds—as we hoped. But loftier embankments meant climbing flood crests, by reason of further confining the waters, until our levee system becomes inadequate to carry such floods as are now predicted. The clearing of more and more lands above us, with a scientific perfection of drainage, tends to throw water more rapidly into the channel so that with the same amount of rainfall as before, we must expect still greater floods.

Along the river's edge lie certain lowlands, natural basins for the stoppage and storage of water, like the St. Francis basin and mouth of the Yazoo. Many of these, too many, have been closed, adding their contents to a full channel when the levees cannot hold another foot. Neither can levees be lifted many more feet.

There comes a limit to the height of levee building, a limit that we have pretty nearly reached. These ridges are made of soft earth and rest upon soft earth, oftentimes crossing treacherous sloughs and hidden sandbars which the river has filled over and concealed. If we keep piling more weight and more weight upon mushy foundations, some of them must ultimately sink.

For these and other reasons our levees must not be elevated to more dangerous heights. The moderate raise now planned, an average of perhaps three feet, is knowingly insufficient to hold a superflood.

If the levees alone might not hold the highest imaginable water, and if some of it must burst loose somewhere, it seems common sense to discharge a portion where an overflow would do least harm. So "The Adopted Plan" proposed exactly that, to provide an outlet and relieve the channel. This outlet became known as the "fuse plug" at Cypress Creek, Arkansas, diverting a certain amount of flowage by way of Boeuf River Basin into the Gulf. The fuse plug scheme aroused such local antagonism that the point of outlet was changed by the recent Overton Bill. Under the new law, instead of Cypress Creek, the spillway will leave the main channel near

Eudora, Arkansas, bearing the surplus of any super-flood through Southern Louisiana, with restraining dykes on either side, and dumping it safely into the sea at Morgan City, one hundred miles west of New Orleans.

New Orleans must be made secure; a crevasse here, to say nothing of human life, would cost many times the millions spent on prevention.

According to expert opinion that city can be defended against any possible water. An outlet at Eudora is the first step, then a magnificent achievement now complete at Bonnet Carre.

Bonnet Carre is twenty-five miles above the Crescent City where dangerous waters may be shunted into Lake Pontchartrain which communicates with the Gulf.

Bonnet Carre Spillway is so designed as to give absolute control of the discharge, much or little as may seem prudent. Whenever a rising river threatens New Orleans, sluice gates will be opened, taking off sufficient excess to prevent the crest from mounting above twenty feet at New Orleans. Past records indicate that about once in every five years it may be necessary to open the gates. At this rate a deposit of silt in Lake Pontchartrain may average 1/32 of an inch a year.

Levees along the main river are now finished, while some work still remains to be done on the tributaries. Water that formerly submerged vast areas in five states is being carried off without a drop of overflow. When the Eudora Spillway, or flowage channel, becomes an accomplished fact, engineers believe that King Cotton's Valley will be safe as Pike's Peak, barring accidents or an unthinkable combination of catastrophies.

XV

HUNGER FOR THE RAW

THE small farmer, as well as big properties like Panther Burn, must compete with a cotton-growing world. Wise men in the game keep their eyes open to see what other lands are doing.

The Briton has always looked ahead, seeking to grow fibre under his own flag, and declare a commercial independence of our southern fields. More than a century ago British agricultural experts were stimulating production in India, which dwindled in the forties and fifties, largely because of lax native methods. Civil War in America spurred the Briton again, in the West Indies, Africa, everywhere he could get cotton without having to run the blockade of Union war vessels.

We speak now of 1910, to show the situation in contrast with what has since occurred. The cotton-hungry Briton sailed every sea, his cork helmet disappeared over the rim of every horizon. With portable bathtub he invaded every jungle. Through savage lands ran a persistent trail worn by the feet of cotton seekers who were not making tracks for fun. They were hungry for the raw, for raw cotton to feed their ravenous mills in Lancashire. Lancashire mills employed a half million operatives, and cotton spinning next to agriculture constituted the chief industry of Great Britain. The business had become insecure, for British looms then depended almost entirely upon America.

Years before our Civil War they jogged along in what seemed to them the safest of ruts, using a fibre not one ounce of which could be grown at home. In those days, however, the crop was ample to meet all demands, and Lancashire bought cotton at its own figure. Spindles whirred full speed, and a steady jingle of guineas convinced Lancashire that its industry was founded on a rock.

The first rude jostle came in shape of hostilities in America (1861) when a blockade cut off three-fourths of their supply, threw 250,000 operatives out of work, with 165,000 others only partially employed. At that time Lancashire needed about two and three quarter million bales of American cotton and could not get it.

Towards the close of the Civil War staple in New York averaged one dollar per pound, or much higher, and spinners want cheap cotton. Until the eighties an average price held itself above ten cents, then fell so low that multitudinous new uses were invented to consume a six cent commodity. From 1895 to 1909 British mills increased their spindles seventeen per cent. Continental Europe increased 39 per cent, while Uncle Sam himself entered the field and added no less than 72 per cent to his capacity.

In 1865-6 America spun two-thirds of a million bales, which by 1907-8 had risen to more than four million bales, until home consumption equaled what had been our entire American crop for any one year up to 1879. In other words, unless our crop itself had been phenomenally increased, at this time there would have been no cotton whatever remaining for export.

From 1892 to 1901 while Lancashire increased 2¼ per cent and the Continent 31 per cent, consumption in the United States jumped more than 60 per cent. England barely kept pace with its normal growth of population.

These American leaps and bounds staggered the British spinner. Coming forward to 1909 Lancashire gets another nervous shock when its consumption actually fell below the figures of 1891. The Continent was then taking more than six million bales, an increase of 50 per cent, while American mills consumed about five million bales, an expansion of 100 per cent since 1891. The United States now used not only all of its own best cotton, but actually imported long staple from Egypt, snatching the finest of fibre from the British Lion's mouth.

An enormous jump in cotton production had not been sufficient to supply the expanding Continental and American mills, in addition to those of Lancashire. A few seasons ago seven million American bales were supposed to glut the world. In 1909 with nearly twice as great a yield, a cotton famine threatened, only temporarily relieved by such a crop as the big one of 1911. Lancashire saw no remedy in the future, and the master spinner warned his associates that unless a larger supply of raw material could be procured from wider-producing areas, the industry of Lancashire was doomed.

Where must he look for expansion? Not to India as he saw it in 1910. India had been planting more than twenty million acres, about two-thirds the acreage of the United States, and her yield averaged 90 pounds to an acre, say, three and a half million standard bales. Indian cotton is too coarse for Lancashire looms except in rougher fabrics; for better goods it must be spun in connection with long staple. Though the extent of the India crop varies but little every year, the staple seemed to be getting worse. In addition to this, India became a greater and greater consumer, her own mills absorbing 20 per cent more cotton than they did ten years ago. Exports went principally to Japan and the Continent, Germany being the best customer.

An even greater difficulty was presented by lax methods of native cultivation, and their habits were not subject to change.

Egypt promised no material increase in production. Every acre was already doing what it could, and there was no additional land. By scientific selection of seed, artificial manuring and modern agricultural methods, a somewhat better crop might be grown. The Egyptian fellah made his record spurt during our American Civil War, played his limit at the start and kept nothing in reserve. Egypt's enormous area is mostly desert; only the Nile Valley could be cultivated—and the Nile Valley is not capable of enlargement.

Lancashire could not look to China's twelve hundred thousand bales or to Japan's six thousand. Chinese cotton went chiefly to the Mikado's mills, which also consumed four hundred thousand bales of Indian and two hundred thousand bales of American cotton.

One big idea had always persisted in the British spinner's mind—that cotton must be grown within the Empire, planted beneath the Union Jack, guarded by her far-flung battle line and freighted home in British bottoms. This was a job for which the spinners straightway organized the "British Cotton Growing Association," born May 1902 at Manchester.

The field was broad. According to reports from expert scouts Britain saw a cotton zone that girdled this rotund earth from the collar bone to the knee, from 40 degrees north to 40 degrees south. The north line of this parallel of latitude enclosed nearly the whole of Korea, it passed through China at Peking and out of Asia at Constantinople. It slices off the southern part of Greece, Italy and Spain, piercing through the United States at Philadelphia and Indianapolis.

The southern parallel includes the whole of

Africa, and all of South America except lower Patagonia. It takes in Australia and the Islands of the sea. In fact omits nothing of the British Empire except the home nest and Canada.

Within these limits British Cotton Growers concocted a mighty project, nothing more nor less than a vast experimental farm where cheap cotton must be, can be, shall be grown under the banner of His Most Gracious Majesty.

British experimenters hustled in dead earnest. Before this they had wandered about aimlessly, punching holes in the horizon with golf balls and dawdling over Turkish cigarettes. Now with a capital of one-half million sterling, and three-fourths of creation for a cotton patch, spinners' agents had no leisure to loaf with perky subalterns and cuss the War Office. Grim men went forth with pockets full of cottonseed, while a paternal government provided every facility to raise grub for their infant industry, free land, free freight, experts for educational and experimental work, free seed, free plows, free gins, free presses. The government also advanced ten thousand guineas yearly.

First the Association thought of reviving the growth of cotton in countries where it had been cultivated long before the plant was discovered in America.

In many British colonies cotton grows absolutely wild, like the natives. Missionaries of the mill experimented in every continent on the globe and most of the islands. They literally sifted every soil and made chemical analyses of the earth. Take that vast Sudan—Fuzzy Wuzzy country—where pagan black soldiers enable British Christians to rule over Mohammedans. Part of this Sudan was fitted for cotton, which grows of its own accord in spite of local negligence. Tradition identifies the Sudan as the original home of Egyptian fibre, but the present Sudanese prefer a variety that gives no trouble, just as they prefer everything else without trouble. Indigenous cotton is a nappy stuff suited to nappy-headed needs, and natives don't worry about Egyptian staple.

Labor too is scarce since the Mahdi and Khakifa killed off 75 per cent of the tribesmen.

Along the Atbara and the Nile, and in those unmeasured plains of the Gezira, are millions of acres where cotton would grow. The Gezira lies between the White Nile and the Blue, with a soil resembling that of our Yazoo-Mississippi Delta. This triangle is supposed to contain about one-third as many arable acres as Egypt, and might produce some seven hundred thousand Egyptian bales. This must be done by irrigation. The lands lie ideally with sufficient slope to be supplied by the Blue Nile, richest of all fertilizing agencies. Soil, climate and water are possible in the Gezira; but men, ah, there's the rub, to get men.

It was hoped that raising the dam at Assouan still higher might encourage cotton growing. Such also was the hope when that marvelous railroad crossed the Nubian Desert from Old Berber to the Red Sea at Suakim. The railroad is now a fact, but industrious cotton producers still remain a thing of faith.

One plantation in that country actually showed accomplishment. This property is called Zeidab, located near the mouth of the Atbara River where it enters the Nile. Some of its land yields 1300 pounds of unginned cotton to the acre, with an average of 400 pounds of lint. Other acres, better cultivated, yield as much as 700 pounds of lint. In 1910 Zeidab managers computed that an average tenant cultivating ten acres should produce

4,500 pounds of lint @ 25¢	$1,125.00
9,000 pounds of seed	150.00
	$1,275.00
Cost of ginning and baling	$ 35.00
Freight to Alexandria	85.00
Rent at £4 sterling per acre	200.00
Cultivation and picking	150.00
	$470.00

On ten acres of cotton the tenant should make a net profit of $805.

Rent is here estimated at about one-third of what is charged for the same character of land in lower Egypt. Egyptian lands now rent for less in Egypt.

Nyasaland lies near the east coast of Africa just

below Pupanganda—if that means anything. British spinners formerly called it "The Lancashire Hope," "ample and fertile acres, a large and intelligent population." What more could the planter want? Dr. Livingstone discovered that Nyasaland cotton was being cultivated, but the natives were not. In 1903, their exports were worth $15,000, and five years later had risen to $140,000. Spinners built a railroad and started steamboats, but nothing to alarm America has yet happened.

Uganda is exactly in the middle of the inkiest spot in the blackest section of darkest Africa. Sir Samuel Baker branded it "an internal hell and external nuisance," which formed the British pretence for annexation. Years ago some Arab traders introduced cotton seed that grew carelessly, just as negroes grew. Huge sums were spent fostering the industry, but they seemed to get nowhere in particular.

The trouble all over Africa is that natives live so easily that it distracts their attention from hard work. Experiments in Nigeria tell the same story, so does Natal, Cape Colony, Rhodesia, Australia, the Transvaal, Ceylon, Cypress, Borneo.

Lagos on the west coast is another instance. As far back as 1869, that island exported 77,000 pounds sterling worth of cotton, but the reopening of our southern fields after the Civil War killed their trade. The same stoppage occurred in the Fiji Islands. British West Indies formerly supplied 70 per cent of Lancashire cotton, but our southern states entered the competition and a West Indian sugar industry developed that was more profitable to the islander.

In six years of effort, up to the close of 1909, the British Cotton Growing Association, by scraping around from Tasmania to Timbuctoo, succeeded in producing a total of 83,000 bales, which was about one-thirtieth of what was required for their mills.

This is a mere thumbnail sketch, but representing a viewpoint of 1910. We shall come back to it and discuss what happened when American acreage was restricted by law.

XVI

PISTOLS, PANIC, AND PROSPERITY

TO comprehend the dependence of "spots" on "futures" we might recall the bewildering adventures of Wash Johnson when Cotton Exchanges slammed their doors in his face.

To begin with, Wash wasn't studying about the white fellow, had never laid eyes on him, for Wash was busy tending twenty acres of land when that foreigner commenced foolin' with a pistol and shot the rations out of Brother Johnson's mouth.

A totally unexpected trigger trick. Wash didn't see the gunman, the gunman couldn't see him; and it took a long-range six-shooter to kill Wash Johnson's commissary account at a distance of eight thousand miles. For the shooting took place at Sarajevo in Bosnia, while Wash was just getting ready to pick cotton on Colonel Woodville's plantation in Mississippi.

The same bullet incidentally slew an archduke, which might be proper and regular, as Wash didn't believe in game laws. One word in Europe brought on another and started a free-for-all scrap which starved Wash Johnson for a while, then landed him on the front seat of a brand new automobile.

It required two years, however, before Wash got

to running his own "Tin Lizzie" with a grin that advertised every whitewashed tooth in his face. Instead of firing up with corn and pulling the bell cord over old Beck, he tilted a rakish hat to one side and cussed the speed limit.

After the sudden flare-up in Bosnia, things on the plantation got so ticklish that nobody knew which way to jump. The Colonel scratched his head, Wash scratched his cotton, and negroes scratched mightily to raise hogs and hominy.

It reads like a Munchausen yarn, how an irresponsible fanatic in the Balkans could shoot the rations out of Wash Johnson's mouth, and then, by nigger luck, bestow upon Wash an automobile that he had never dreamed of owning.

The story should begin with "once upon a time," but it doesn't. It opens on a fixed date, June 28th, 1914, when a student assassinated the Archduke Franz Ferdinand of Austria, which did not immediately affect the cotton market.

All his life Colonel Woodville had suspected that whenever British mills wanted to pay less for his crop they whispered in hoarse tones, "Europe trembles on the brink of war"—a bogey man that depressed the price.

Despite the wrangling of European diplomats, for a time cotton held its own, the average per bale for July 1914 being $67.

July 28th, just a month after the first shot, Colonel Rye sat on his front gallery smiling at a thousand

acres of the finest staple that a crow ever flew over.
He expected to gin six hundred and fifty bales, worth
$40,000. Tenants would have money to pay rent
and commissary accounts, with cash for popcorn and
dirigible balloons at Christmas. Thirteen-cent cotton was a fairy godmother to pacify the factor, pay
the merchant, and settle with the bank.

Colonel Rye eased down in a rocking chair and
resumed his inspection of railway folders. His
daughters were going away—New York, London,
Paris. Early winter with friends in Rome—then
back to the plantation for an old-fashioned Christmas. The Colonel felt good.

Wash Johnson was likewise feeling good. He
had "laid by" his crop, ended all labor for the year
until picking time. So he grinned at the Colonel
as he approached, and the Colonel smiled back.

"Good evenin', Cunnel."

"Good evening, Wash. What do you want?"

"Cunnel, dese niggers is fixin' to hold a festerval,
an' I 'zires a new suit o' clo'es."

"Why don't you go get them?"

"Dat's what I aims to do. Gimme a order on de
sto', please, suh, an' some shoes wid a hat, an' things."

"That's right, Wash. Dress up. Dress up fine."

The boss scribbled a carte blanche order and Wash
had already started off with it when Dr. Scott came
whirling through the big gate and sprang excitedly
from his dust-covered automobile. Unfortunately
Wash remained to hear the news.

"Colonel," the Doctor exclaimed, "war's broke out in Europe."

"What?"

"Austria has invaded Serbia. Russia's mobilizing. Germany's marching into France, and—"

Wash Johnson stood with mouth wide open, listening to the white folks without comprehending what it was all about. Both the white men realized that war, with a general stoppage of trade, meant six cent cotton, five cent cotton, cotton of no value— inevitable ruin.

Ruin tomorrow signified nothing to Wash Johnson if today he held the Colonel's order for a suit of clothes, and the commissary stood open for him to draw rations. He had made a pretty good crop, which at 13 cents should pay his debts and leave a substantial number of dollars for holiday whisky. So Wash never pestered his head about Europe until Colonel Woodville reached out for that scrap of paper representing a new suit, took it away from Wash and tore it up.

"Hole on, Cunnel, hole on. Dem's my new clo'es."

"Got to wear your old ones, Wash."

"How come?"

"Wash," he said, "we'll have to go mighty slow. Nothing but meat, meal and molasses, darn little of that."

The colonel rose thoughtfully, turned into the house and notified his daughters to unpack their trunks. No travel that summer.

Rumors of war had always beat down the value of cotton. This was worse than rumor—it was a wreck.

Not that Colonel Rye thought only of his pecuniary interest. Far from it. He had traveled extensively, been educated at Heidelberg and lived in France. During his own boyhood he had experienced all the horrors of civil strife. His heart throbbed in sympathy with devastated Belgium, for slaughtered Serbia, for brave lads slain. We shall not speak of these, only of cotton.

On July 30th, 1914, exchanges closed in New York and London; next day the Cotton Exchange suspended at New Orleans. Europe blazed up like flames crackling through dry canebrakes. The Germans marched across Belgium, and it was just as if those khaki columns had gone tramping across Ruthven's unpicked fields. Monstrous cannon battering at Liege, were also battering the price of cotton. And worse: it speedily developed that they were confronting a crop of seventeen millions, instead of fourteen and a half.

This unprecedented production could find no outlet. Over 60 per cent of it was formerly exported, and these dammed-up millions of bales must now be tiered in gin sheds, warehouses, railroad platforms, scarcely worth transportation or storage. American mills could only nibble at such a vast accumulation, and what they spun would be at their own figure.

The financial world tied itself into hard knots. A congestion of cotton causes a tighter congestion of cash.   Normal exports—say, nine million bales— would bring back more than $600,000,000. Whoever does not realize that cotton is a potent factor in national development need only try to finance a new venture when this returning flow of southern cash is shut off.   The stoppage of $600,000,000 strangled every financial artery in America.

Everything halted right where it was, everything but cotton, and cotton kept dropping like a drunken man tumbling down a stair to which there seemed no bottom.   It tumbled from 13½ to 6½, with scattering sales at 6 cents, 5½ and even 5 cents. Soon it might reach the all-time low of 4½ cents in 1845.

When exchanges closed there was no such thing as quotations. Nobody had even a guess, and stampeded holders sacrificed their cotton. Even if the seas had been safe with all ports open, ample ships and easy money, our crops could not have moved because there was no future market.

An average man fails to differentiate between the legitimate and the speculative, just as Wash Johnson cannot understand why the closing of exchanges would hinder the clerk at Colonel Woodville's commissary from issuing regular rations. Bear in mind that our colored friend raises the only crop that the producer never consumes. Wheat, corn, hay, chickens, hogs, are partly consumed on the farm; but Wash can't eat cotton and can't wear it until

somebody else runs it through a mill. Hence Wash
has to sell. Now let us see how future markets affect
the sale. Suppose that negroes go crazy over a certain calico, the streakity, stripety kind, and Wash
Johnson's wife demands it from the plantation commissary. Other black women throughout our Cotton Belt ask for the same patterns. Inquiries pour
in upon jobbers who write to wholesalers at New
York.

The wholesaler goes to a mill treasurer in Fall
River, Massachusetts, and says, "My customers are
inquiring for certain calicos. At what figure can
you furnish them?"

The treasurer knows the price at which he can
buy cotton to make these goods. But fibre may advance five cents a pound before he needs it six
months hence. So he may do one of two things:
first, contract with a responsible southern shipper to
sell actual cotton for future delivery; or second, buy
a future contract.

It might require several days to consummate his
deal with a shipper, whereas a future contract may
be made in ten minutes, and the wholesaler is waiting for an answer. Therefore, the treasurer elects
to buy October futures now quoted at 12.36 and wires
his broker to purchase six hundred bales. On the
basis of raw material at 12.36 he agrees with the
wholesaler to manufacture so many bolts of cloth for
delivery on specified dates. The wholesaler in turn

is now able to quote southern jobbers, who make prices to country stores.

But suppose instead of buying a future contract the mill treasurer buys actual cotton for future delivery. He wires his correspondent at Vicksburg, Mississippi, asking an offer on six hundred bales of given grade and staple to be delivered in August, September and October. His Vicksburg correspondent knows today's price, but has no assurance for tomorrow, and would not chance the loss of ten dollars a bale. However the future market is open, so he offers the mill treasurer six hundred bales at a certain figure, which is accepted. To hedge against fluctuations, the southern shipper immediately buys six hundred bales of futures, which protects him against a rise in the market until he can purchase spots.

This being done the correspondent goes to Ruthven Plantation and contracts to buy the entire crop—including Wash Johnson's ten bales.

While Cotton Exchanges were closed such a transaction could not be carried through, and Colonel Woodville's crop must remain unsold.

At the beginning of the World War, even if the seas had been safe, there would have been great difficulty in moving cotton. Trading was done on the wildest hazard, buying at blind prices with the hope of selling again at unknown figures. Banks declined to finance such speculations and conservative business men kept out of the market.

In June 1914 a certain New Orleans exporter sold a spinner in Europe ten thousand bales at an average price of 12¾ cents for delivery, we will say, in December. As the deal showed a profit to the exporter, he insured that profit by a purchase of futures.

In September this exporter bought ten thousand bales of actual cotton at six cents, and had apparently made a profit of $337,500, but his future contracts were outstanding and he could not get rid of them, was forced to gamble whether he wanted to or not, and each decline of one cent per pound cost him $60,000.

If he could pay the present loss on his futures and collect the profit on his spots, that would put him $37,500 to the good, but he couldn't turn loose his future contract because the exchanges had shut their doors.

Other exporters in the same predicament were anxious to cover with spots at prevailing low prices, provided they could liquidate their future contracts. Not being able to do this kept them out of the market, and forced values to still lower levels.

By this time—November 1914—the new crop was being ginned. A bale now represented $37 instead of $67, so the planter must convert nearly twice as many of them into cash to meet his obligations. Under the weight dumped upon it, prices kept dropping.

When exchanges reopened middling sold at seven

cents. For a generation spinners had never bought so cheap, and could make quick profits on manufactured goods. They rushed into the market; so did the speculators, which added a tremendous buying power. Yet this buying power confronted many elements of uncertainty and apprehension. German raiders prowled the seas and American exporters could not guess how far their blockade of British ports might prove effective. On November first, the Germans won a naval victory off the coast of Chili, and cotton prices sagged, to rise again on November 6th when the *Emden* was destroyed. Two months later the German fleet was sunk near the Falkland Islands, and floating commerce became safer.

At this crisis a new factor stepped into the picture and revolutionized the movement of cotton. Old systems were wiped out when the Federal Reserve Bank began operations in 1914, supplying money that enabled a producer of agricultural commodities to sit tight in the boat and sell his cotton or wheat as needed, not in overwhelming waves that would burst the bottom out of any market. This had a wonderful effect in steadying farm prices.

From 7 cents, in November 1914, spot cotton began to climb by its own power. There was no recognized bull clique as in previous advancing years. Speculators followed the market in a timid way instead of leading it. Rumors leaked out of big munitions contracts, orders for clothing, tentage material and the like. Quotations went up and up so strongly that prices continued to mount in spite of a seventeen million bale crop, the largest ever grown, when only fourteen and a half had been expected.

During July 1914, before the crash of the war, the average price of a bale was $67, then the sickening slump, and not for two full years did values reach the peak from which they'd toppled, $67 per bale.   Soon afterward another rise began for substantial reasons:

Prior to July 31st, 1916, few observers looked for a consumption of more than thirteen and a half million bales.   On that date Mr. Henry G. Hester, Secretary of the New Orleans Cotton Exchange, issued his statement showing a fourteen and three quarter million bale consumption of American cotton.   This made every spinner sit up and take notice.   Spots hadn't near reached the top of their pole, and started on a more spectacular climb, which by October 25th, 1916, had added $28.10 to the value of every bale.

Occasionally, when something extraordinary happened at the seat of war, cotton might slide back, but in the main it kept on climbing.

The rise was different from all speculative advances because it came at a time when increased prices went directly to Colonel Woodville and Wash Johnson.   Never before, except once, had there been a speculative rise while cotton yet remained in farmers' hands.   Now he got full benefit.

Few growers had considered how much of their

cotton would go into war material for millions and millions of tents, to replace the destruction of automobile tires, absorbent cotton in hospitals. A single discharge of one big gun on board the *Queen Elizabeth* burned up six hundred pounds of Wash Johnson's crop.

Remember, we deal only with cotton prices, not with a southern planter's feeling towards the blood and agony of crucified mankind.

November 1916. Again Colonel Woodville sat upon his front gallery, just where he'd been sitting when he got news of the war. He smiled to himself at the story a garage mechanic told him.

One of the Ruthven tenants had smashed his car and taken it to the shop.

"Boss," he inquired, "how long befo' you kin fix it?"

"Not until Monday morning."

"Lordee, boss, I'm bleeged to have my otto on Sunday. I loves to ride an' keep a-ridin' all day Sunday."

"Sorry, but it won't be ready until Monday."

The negro glanced around, then pointed to a little road louse in the corner, "Whose car is dat?"

"Mine."

"Does you aim to sell it?"

"Yes, if I got my price."

"What's it wuth?"

"Three hundred dollars."

"All right, suh, I'll jest buy dis car whilst I'm waitin' fer mine."

The bale that two years ago had sold for $37 now brought $95, and some of Ruthven's high grade long staple brought $180. The roads buzzed with Tin Lizzies. The blacksmith shop was piled up with shattered wrecks. Grinning negroes wore bandages and swapped details of accidents.

While Colonel Woodville sat there studying over all that had happened, here came Wash Johnson whose order for new clothes the boss had torn up two years ago. Wash was covered with dust and showed a bloody gash across his forehead.

"Wash," the Colonel asked, "what's the matter?"

"Dat fool nigger, Elder Spriggs, wouldn't gimme no road, so I knocked him out of it."

"Hurt anybody?"

"Not overly much, suh. Dey toted him home. Cunnel, what's de mos' 'stravagant ottermobile I kin buy?"

"Did you wreck yours?"

"Huh, 'twon't nary one o' dem cars do fer kindlin' wood. Blacksmith say he can't ontangle 'em. I wants a 'stravagant car."

"An extravagant car? Why?"

" 'Cause my wife's got a lot o' po' kin folks in de hills. Dey heerd I was rich an' come down to stay wid us. I aims to spend my money an' git shet o' dem lazy niggers."

2

Pigs an' chickens hustle,
Scramble out de road;
Bunch o' cotton croppers
Ridin' in a Fode.

Pack 'em on de cushions,
Jam de runnin' bode;
Chunks of grinnin' happiness
In a shiny Fode.

Crank her up with muscle,
Hit de grit fer town;
Never mind de rattle
While de wheel turns round.

Won't eat nary tater,
Neither meat an' greens;
Wash is at de steerer,
Eatin' sardines.

'Nother car behind him;
Don't you let 'em pass;
Beat 'em to de crossin',
Steppin' on de gas.

Skid around de corners,
Bridges at a jump;
Hit a little bull calf!
Biff! Bang! Bump!

Smash ag'inst de phone pole!
Tumble in de ditch!
What t'ell's de diff'ence?
Ev'ybody's rich.

Rich—that's the hilarious idea! All the King's children had made bumper crops; their fields were piled like snowdrifts with fluffy cotton at twenty cents a pound and upward. So Wash Johnson grins upon a world that grins back at him, with teeth whiter than his cotton. Silver jingles merrily in his jeans; money to buy clothes and gingersnaps, to have his portrait enlarged in crayon, with a gilt frame.

During a few weeks of scatteration no luxury will be too expensive for Wash. He'll skylark through lavish holidays, squander every cent of his cash, and on the first of February go shuffling into the plantation store to draw rations on credit. But look at the fun he had. As compared with Wash in his brief day of prosperity, a drunken sailor looks conservative. Sailors spend in driblets, while Wash lets the hide go with the horns and tallow.

His kinky head is full of wheels. He craves to ride, to ride fast. The present owner of any rattletrap automobile need only limp to the nearest gin and the nearest Wash will buy it.

After he cashes his check from the first ginning, Wash astonishes the store loafers by appearing in a huge asthmatic limousine. For miles the negroes hear him coming and assemble on the gallery, which tickles Wash mightily. He doesn't hanker to arrive in silence and obscurity, but craves the biggest, noisiest car on the plantation, exhumed from its forgotten burial, a relic of 1902. Out steps Wash, his hat cocked to one side and a gold band cigar in the southwest corner of his face. For this antique he probably paid fifty dollars cash, giving notes for more, and saved its former owner the cost of hauling away so much junk.

An investigator who may be curious to study the difference between hard times and flush times need only take a road on either bank of the Mississippi River, in Mississippi or Louisiana, on a red-hot Sunday when every negro is abroad. To each fifty miles of highway he will observe fifty Wash Johnsons halted at the roadside, "fixin' de Fode." A scorching sun beats down upon them, sweat spatters on the gravel; they wave their jubilant hands at other Wash Johnsons who go dashing past. Hammers jangle on the Sabbath air, and dust clouds settle on their dappled faces. Anybody except a hard-boiled southerner might pity these poor creatures mending their inner tubes while the thermometer sizzled at 105. Save your sympathy. Wash wouldn't consider patching his tube in a back yard where nobody could see him. He desires the publicity and is radiantly happy, puffing a cigar while he fixes his Fode. Wash would rather tinker with a rattletrap than to ride in it. Not that he's a mechanical genius any more than Sonny Boy who punches holes in his drum to discover where the fuss comes from.

Planters always prefer that Wash shouldn't buy an automobile while half his cotton remains in the field. When he's poor his landlord refuses credit for anything appertaining to an auto, tires, gas or parts. But for these few riotous weeks Wash asks no credit, no favors. He has money, real money, making music in his pocket, and itches to spend it. He won't hit another lick of work until he's broke his Fode and broke himself, so the landlord shrugs his shoulders and figures like this: "Wash is going to throw away his money anyhow. Town gamblers will get it, or criminal lawyers. He will rarely buy land or anything that does him permanent good."

"Very well," the boss considers, "Let him chuck it at the jay birds; the sooner the better."

Before any coiner of economic proverbs throws rocks at Wash Johnson for extravagance, let him stand for a moment in Wash's tattered shoes. This negro is nothing but a child—a big black child— with no heredity of sustained effort behind him, no training, no background. True, he never risks an injury to his constitution by arduous toil, but he does work—some. And through bad year after bad year he didn't have one lonesome nickel to clink against its fellow. So in a prosperous season with half his crop ungathered he is bedazzled to find himself clear of debt; which pleases the landlord far more than it relieves Wash. On top of that the boss has given him a fabulous check, an inexhaustible fortune of two hundred and thirty-seven dollars. What's Wash going to do? Sink it in a savings bank? Buy land? Sensible clothing? No sirree! No more than a boy will spend his firecracker money

for a pair of shoes at Christmas. Childlike, he
means to have a fling, be a sport, to "show dese niggers a tech o' high life." Maybe if Poor Richard
had stagnated through previous lean years with
Wash Johnson he might forget that a penny saved
is a penny earned, and kick up his frisky heels
against a pair of startled coattails.

Wash loves to buy, buy, buy, to buy anything—
a shelf-worn submarine, a wooden leg, a set of gold
teeth—and revels in the splendor of disbursement.
Around such a versatile purchaser the fakers swarm
thicker than flies at a molasses bung. Slick tongues
sell him chests full of medical concoctions. For one
hundred bucks he acquires a snakeskin belt steeped
in magic vinegar to restore lost vitality. He invests
in rugs with blue roses, and accident insurance with
red seals. He buys chunks and chunks of happiness.
What t'ell's the difference? Everybody's rich, so
Wash Johnson fills his car jam full of friends, buys
a dollar's worth of bananas and steps on the gas:

> All his tires poppin'
> Underneath the load;
> Slingin' out banana peel
> Up and down de road.

XVII

MECHANICAL COTTON PICKERS

THE itinerant corn doctor went slipping about, setting up a soap box wherever he could, and hawking his nostrum. Late one afternoon while haranguing a crowd of tenants behind the gin house, he noticed an old man to whom he'd sold a box of salve.

"Friend," the quack called out to his customer, "kindly step forward and tell these good people how my salve took off your corn."

"Yas, suh," the negro hobbled painfully on his crutches and testified, "dat stuff sho did take off my corn. Sho did, suh. An' tuk de toe wid it."

That's always been the hitch with mechanical cotton pickers. Many devices would take off cotton, some cotton, but also took sticks, leaves, bolls, with chunks of the plantation, and churned everything together like a concrete mixer.

For near a century since Whitney's gin became an accomplished fact, the inventive genius of America has studied this problem of picking cotton by machinery, and still seems baffled by its difficulties. From about 1850 up to date, more than eight hundred devices have passed through our patent office, an average of ten per year, each in turn being pro-

claimed as the ultimate achievement to revolution-
ize the cotton industry. None, however, have proven
measurably successful, and not one has established
itself in use. Inventors tried every imaginable contraption; some were operated by one man on foot,
others required cumbersome machines drawn by
mules or tractors. We've had the vacuum-cleaner
type, the endless band studded with spikes, twisters,
snatchers, pullers, grabbers, and all, without excep-
tion, took the toe with it.

Silky staples of the delta must be gathered free
from trash or dirt which lowers the grade and makes
it worth far less money. Two human pickers may
work side by side in the same field where one of
them seizes everything he can grab, while the other
selects only lint; then the well-picked bale sells for
ten or twenty dollars more. It may happen that a
big economy in the cost of picking by hand would
be offset by a bigger loss in grade.

At 75 cents per hundred pounds, it costs about
$9.50 to gather a bale of cotton. Suppose a machine
gathers it for $2.50, thereby saving $7; but suppose
the machine-picked bale is trashy—which heretofore has been the case—it will bring at least $10 less
than the hand-picked bale, and the farmer actually
loses $3.

The cotton plant does not grow to uniform height
or breadth. On sorry land in the hills we have
the "bumble bee" kind that may not rise up to a
man's knee, while on alluvial river soil the plant

may grow eight feet high. Sometimes there's almost as great a difference between plants in the same field where human pickers stoop to pluck lint from a boll only a few inches from the ground, yet must not miss another boll two feet above their heads. One boll dangles at the far end of a branch, another hides on a short stem against the stalk. The picker must get both.

Neither do all bolls burst open at one time, but first mature on bottom limbs where fluffy lint hangs out. At the middle of the stalk, bolls are green or turning brown, but still solid, and top blossoms, if left alone by the weevil and the frost, will in time produce fibre. We find open bolls, green bolls and blossoms all at once on the same plant, so hand pickers usually go through a field three times to get the bottom, the middle, and the top crop.

Because of these difficulties experienced planters continue to be skeptical. Yet this is a day of miracles in which human intelligence has conquered the air and navigated the underseas. Talking pictures, radio, television—science changes the impossibilities of yesterday into commonplace utilities of today, and he would be a rash prophet who predicts, "It can't be done."

Every year or so within human memory it is announced that a cotton picker has at last been perfected, and growers from all over the Belt are invited to witness its tryout. On a specially prepared field, under ideal conditions, the machine does pick cotton. Farmers gather round and applaud, while public thinkers begin to theorize on effects so far-reaching that the thinker gets scared. A cheap machine might overturn the entire structure of King Cotton by gathering such unconsumable masses as to smother the world in lint at five cents a pound, at two cents, at half a cent, no bottom to the price. Regardless of how inexpensive the process, cotton might not be worth hauling from the field.

Again, the theorist considers that machinery might ensure America's predominance over foreign countries whose people abhor such contraptions.

Suppose the picker costs so much that it could be used only by rich planters, and automatically drove the small farmer from competition because he couldn't work by hand against machinery, or live on seven to ten bales of cotton at the price to which machine production would lower it? And where could millions of plantation negroes go if thrust out from their time-honored occupation?

Thinkers of the past had plenty to worry over, then forgot it, because nothing happened. Farmers who had tossed up their hats and cheered did not buy the mechanical picker and use it. So far as this writer can learn, none were ever put on the market with a serious sales campaign, and soon after their tests no more was heard of that particular device.

Remember, we speak only of the past, of the 800 or more attempts that have come and gone. In American work-shops today perhaps many an earnest inventor who knows these obstacles is striving to surmount them.

Half the work of a crop lies in its picking, the output of a tenant being limited not by how much he can plant and cultivate, but by how many bales he can gather. With an efficient machine to do his picking, one agricultural laborer might tend a hundred acres of cotton instead of fifteen.

Suppose some crank bobs up overnight with an amazingly simple contraption which actually selects lint, only lint, and covers twenty, maybe forty acres per day.

Every machine recently projected has been designed for wide stretches of level land, that is for big plantations, whereas it is the one-horse farmer on hillside patches who produces three-fourths of our American crop. So far all machines have been too expensive for him to buy, therefore—we are guessing—75 per cent of our crop must still be gathered by hand unless a mechanical picker moves around and harvests each field as is done by threshing machines. However cheap, that would mean an added cost to the small farmer who does not pay cash for extra labor. With wife and children he gathers his own crop. The family must be fed anyhow, so he probably would not allow them to sit idle while a hired machine picked his cotton. It would save no actual money, and by waiting for the machine, storms might beat his lint into the dirt, decreasing its value by ten to twenty dollars per bale.

Even with a low-cost machine the small farmer might figure that way, and different considerations control the big planter. Assume that his fields are such that tractor or mule-drawn pickers may be used. His tenants are mostly share hands or croppers and, if they do not gather their own crops, must be charged with a proportion of machine cost, which reduces their earnings. Meantime they loaf in the shade and watch the machine because there's no other plantation labor to occupy their time.

A device now attracting public attention was given its second test in September (1936) at the Delta Experiment Station, Stoneville, Mississippi. The station fields are level and broad, with cotton stalks exactly spaced, supposed to furnish ideal conditions for a mechanical picker. Dryness from protracted drouth militated against its full efficiency.

A large gallery of dirt farmers and theoretical experts from several states followed the demonstration of a big machine, like a war tank, that ran by gasoline. Somewhere on the insides about 1400 small spindles revolved rapidly, and being moistened, the lint adheres, is drawn out of its boll and deposited in a sack. That's the idea of Rust's invention, and the audience went away with contrary opinions. According to newspaper accounts most observers agreed that the patent seemed correct in principle, and successfully gathered cotton, but is not yet perfect and needs improvement. Predicting this perfection an enthusiastic editor remarks that

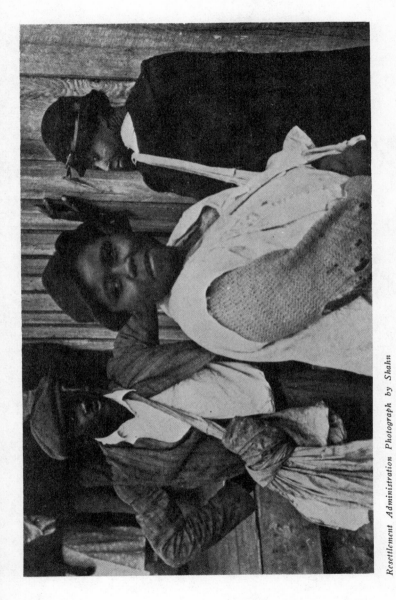

Resettlement Administration Photograph by Shahn

HOW WILL THE MECHANICAL COTTON PICKER AFFECT THEM?

when all faults are remedied, the cotton picker of the future will make today's crudity look like an ox wagon as compared with an airplane.

The consensus of opinion among planters was that Rust's machine is not quite right. Not quite. Their chief objection is expressed by a large operator whose acres are famous for silky staple, "It does not give me the grade."

Grade. That's the essential with him. Year after year he sells to certain spinners practically all the fibre they consume, and must deliver a clean even-running grade, or lose his long-established markets.

Observers of the test pretty well coincide in the statement that too much leaf particles and "stains" are mixed with harvested lint, so lowering its quality that machine-gathered cotton is worth from five to eight dollars less per bale than the same fibre when picked by hand. Its staple is not damaged.

The U. S. Government will now conduct more prolonged tests to determine the relative advantages of hand-picking as compared with machine-picking. Such tests might be illuminating if pursued on two fields that lie side by side and promise the same yield. Let Wash Johnson gather one crop while robot fingers pick the other. The result of hand-picking will be cleaner, higher priced and more of it to the acre, because the machine as yet does not reach every boll, and misses perhaps twenty per cent of lint.

Machine work, however, would be or should be far cheaper than human labor which is now being paid $1.25 to $1.50 per hundred pounds, or about $18 to gather a bale and seed. At the close of the tryout, with each item of debit and credit footed up, comparative figures would show which patch of one hundred acres produced the greater profit.

Anyhow this talk of a successful picker has roused a flock of prophecies all over the United States. Editors devote columns to it, and one usually well-informed journal in the North predicts that Rust's invention will displace five million mules, and twenty-five million acres of western land that now grows delicacies for those mules. The southerner cannot visualize such a calamity for no mule is employed to pick cotton. Old Beck hauls a wagonload to the gin, or drags a plow to break up ground, but Wash Johnson has never trained her to prowl among the stalks and gather lint. Maybe this city editor dreams of a day when all cultivation will be done by tractors, and old Beck given a perpetual cotton holiday.

The threat of a mechanical picker, creating more and widerspread unemployment, has scared a political potentate in Memphis who insists that its use must be prohibited, and such a law can be put across in Tennessee. Old stuff! Moslem caliphs forbade any railroad to enter their dominions or compete with Mahomed's sacred profession of camel-driving; and years ago sob-sisters deplored the plight of "poor seamstresses" when a sewing-machine was invented.

The suggestion from Memphis inspired a Mississippi editor to headline his column with "DARK INVENTIVE DAYS," and scoff, "We had to pinch ourselves when we read that statement to make sure that we were not back in the era when men said that every invention was the work of the devil."

On their side of the controversy Rust Brothers, the patentees, argued that if their home state should bar a mechanical picker, it would handicap Tennessee farmers in competing with foreign producers who offer the machine a ready market. Lot of truth in that, provided the device is practical, and it is now being demonstrated to growers of Soviet Russia.

Planters realize the revolution that must shake our country if a low-priced picker be furnished to small growers who produce the bulk of American cotton. Or an expensive machine, beyond the reach of one-horse farmers, yet adapted to and cheaper for wide areas. In the latter event cotton might become a commodity for mass production only, and drive small fry out of business. We'll cross that bridge when we come to it.

Large plantations would be compelled to make drastic readjustments. Most planters now have dozens of families on their properties whom they could get along without, and there'd be many more if tenants or croppers did no picking. The planter requires negroes, many negroes for certain purposes, such as chopping out young plants. Chopping, however, only employs them for ten or twelve days each season, and unless the boss finds steadier jobs, he couldn't get labor to clean out his cotton.

In the newspapers Rust Brothers announce that they will not lease their picker to any planter unless he obligates himself to take care of labor thrown out of work, and further to create a sort of sinking fund for their benefit.

This sounds vague. How can the planter find work for two hundred tenants or croppers at a season when there's nothing to be done? And if landlords must provide for idle tenants, what's the sense of buying a mechanical picker? Much of this chapter is pure speculation, yet represents what some planters think and say.

Whether or not the Rust machine may solve it, gathering a crop is still the big problem. An innocent bystander on the streets of Boston might imagine that even a negro, when the result of a whole year's toil lies exposed to the weather, would be in a fidget to get it under cover. Wash Johnson knows that autumn storms are coming to blow out his cotton, mixing the staple with leaves and mud and sticks. He understands that cotton picked while it's clean will sell for ten, twenty, forty dollars more to the bale. His field may be white with the prettiest lint that ever delighted a black man's eye, and squawling to come out of the wet. Nevertheless any excuse is sufficient to make Wash run off and leave it.

A tiny cloud arises, one of those half-minute showers that spill forty drops of water. Thirty-nine drops have already been spilled when Colonel Woodville spies Wash straddlewise of a mule, galloping to his cabin.

"Hold on, Wash, hold on," the boss shouts. "What's the matter?"

"I'm runnin' home, suh, to git out o' dis rain."

"But the rain will be over before you get home."

"Yas, suh. Dat's why I'm ridin' so swif'."

When bad weather sets in, the planter frets and urges his tenants to gather their crops, which is a worrisome way of white folks and makes 'em so hard to get along with.

If Wash and family pick steadily six days per week, they can pretty well save their crop, and his landlord wouldn't have to pay a labor agent in town so much per head to send him an assortment of floaters, cook women, odd-job men, all colors and sizes. These are billeted among the plantation cabins, under any roof that affords shelter. Strange faces enliven the monotony of night life, making it a carnival of black and yellow, with dancing, crap shooting, love making and sentimental adventures.

In lean years fifty to seventy-five cents a hundred pounds is the usual rate for picking. But when planters are crying for labor, they pay a dollar and a half a hundred, bunk and rations free. In one respect the negro is like everybody else, and asserts his importance when you can't get along without him. He swaggers and makes demands, demands that are not enforced by bombs or stilettos—but

merely by sitting down.   Fat, black Mammy Liza,
a prominent washerwoman of Vicksburg with two
hefty daughters, went to enjoy a change of air in
the country.   Immediately she realizes that Colonel
Woodville must get his crop picked out, so Mammy
and girls plump their fat selves on Wash Johnson's
gallery and toil not until the landlord sends for them
in an automobile.   Walk to the field?   Not an inch.
They recline in rocking chairs and wait for transportation.   The landlord can't help himself, but
grins and rides them on rubber.

According to ancient custom, when Aunt Liza
had stuffed her sack plum full at fifty cents per hundred, she went waddling like a gingham hippopota-
mus to the scales and got it weighed.   But when paid
a dollar and a half a hundred, with board and lodg-
ing free, she considers it beneath her dignity to
waddle or tote her sack.   The boss must detail a
special negro to come for it.

A novelty in this neck of the woods was an importation of Mexican pickers.   Entire trainloads
were brought from those parts of Texas where crops
had failed.   Many were experienced farmers who
because of drought at home had made no cotton.
To secure this labor Colonel Woodville paid the
transportation one way on their agreement to remain and pick the bulk of his crop.   Mexicans
worked longer hours and more assiduously than
negroes, but did not pick clean.   They grabbed lint,
sticks, leaves, dirt, anything that added weight to

the sacks and swelled their pay envelopes. When Colonel Rye's manager protested, the Mexicans answered, "No savvy"—and went on grabbing. Many had to be sent home, until others comprehended that they must pick only cotton, and omit the stalks.

With sombreros, sashes, gauntlets, high-heeled shoes and clinking spurs, these swarthy fellows and their women added to the picturesqueness of harvest season, but were not permitted to mix, for the Mexican is a crap shooter of renown, and to lock horns with negro dicers might be fatal.

Hundreds of Mexican families annually cross the Rio Grande to pick cotton in Texas, most of it by what they call "snapping," that is by "snapping" off twigs and throwing the entire boll into their sacks. This demands a different kind of ginning to separate lint and trash. During a season of low prices and big crops, Texas "sledded" some of its cotton with a contraption like a steel-tooth sled that caught leaves, stalks, entire plants and dumped them all into a wagon box.

No reverent hand should write an Iliad of the Harvest without a mention of cotton-picking monkeys.

Years ago Captain Mangham had got into a jam, with hundreds of unpicked acres and a shortage of labor. Negroes could not be hired for love nor money, and somebody told him of the trained monkeys in South America, apes with sharp eyes and nimble fingers who worked in gangs of ten, each gang supervised by a human overseer. The desperate planter would try anything once, and cabled for a quick consignment.

One hundred monkeys arrived, vivacious little ring-tail beasts, and when Mangham observed how accurately they picked off one another's fleas, new hope sprang up in his breast. According to instructions, he placed them in the fields, each squad of ten picking under direction of an overseer. It thrilled the planter's soul to watch them begin, possessed of almost human intelligence, and superhuman dexterity. The first day, fine. Second day not so hot. Then a paralysing slump, when those beasts got so darned trifling that instead of ten monkeys working under one overseer, it required all the driving of ten overseers to superintend each gang of one monkey. The experiment failed, as all other picking experiments have failed, except Wash and the sack. Believe it or not, that's Captain Mangham's story.

Hundreds of mechanical pickers have issued their proclamations and hushed, while Colonel Woodville today gathers his lint by the ancient process that men used when Confucius was a kid, the hand-picking method of shirt-tail Hindus and pig-tail Chinamen four thousand years ago.

XVIII

DROSS THAT TURNED TO GOLD

COTTONSEED cluttered the ante-bellum plantations and became a nuisance. Every bale of lint that rolls out from the press leaves behind it more than half a ton of seed, utterly worthless, dross that must be got rid of. The careful planter never allowed accumulations near his gin, but kept negroes and a wagon constantly on the job to haul away seed for burning. Cows were the first Americans to discover its tastiness as food, gorged themselves and died from gossypol poisoning. So the gin was always guarded by a squad of bare-legged black children to drive away cattle.

The planter didn't know what to do with this stuff. He couldn't have it dumped into a creek where it fouled the water and killed fish. Furthermore our criminal laws forbade that under penalty of two hundred dollars' fine. His easiest disposal was by fire at an isolated spot, securely fenced to protect farm animals.

Slipshod management often permitted gin hands to throw out seed as far as a negro could toss them on a shovel, so that vast heaps stacked up and wagons were scarcely able to reach the platform. Once there was a certain planter who for several seasons hadn't bothered to move this refuse until now his gin house looked as if it nestled in a valley surrounded by fuzzy mountain ridges above which only the rooftop showed.

Many times he had strolled out to take a look at the huge barriers, and strolled back again. Now he had to do something and do it quick, for cotton bolls were bursting in his fields and wagons were blocked off from the gin.

"Pomp," he remarked to an old black slave, "it'll take three months to move that pile of seed."

"Den whyn't you move yo' gin house?"

"Hush, Pomp. Nobody ever heard of moving a gin away from the seed."

"Dat's a fack, suh," the stubborn negro persisted. "But nobody ain't never saw sech a pile nigh de gin."

That's exactly what the planter did, dismantled his gin house and set it up at a distance, then burned the seed where they lay, which was cheaper and quicker than moving the seed.

At the outbreak of our Civil War such fires burned almost constantly on every plantation, and destroyed a valuable oil that the Chinese for centuries had been consuming in their lamps. About 1768 an inquisitive scientist in Pennsylvania, named Doctor Otto, pressed a few cottonseed and discovered that they yielded a fatty substance for which nobody could imagine any human use.

Doctor Otto's idea slept twice as long as Rip Van Winkle, although in the meantime four patents had been taken out on crushing processes, and crude mills erected in the South. As early as 1836, oil and cottonseed cake are mentioned as commodities then being carried on steamboats from Natchez to New Orleans.

The oil was originally considered fit for nothing except to make soap, and mighty little of that, so crushing mills did not prosper. Little by little interested manufacturers began hinting at cotton oil as human food, only to meet the same storm of protest that cotton cloth had raised in England. Lard manufacturers and dairy men kicked up such a rumpus and built up such a prejudice against oleomargarine, that demagogues passed laws to tax cotton oil out of American markets. Even today we see new legislation which penalizes people who prefer to eat vegetable oils rather than animal fats.

France was less squeamish about oleomargarine, and about 1865 commissioned one Hypolite Mige to see how far it might be used as a butter substitute for the poor. Professor Mige by his experiments developed a substance that kept so much better and sweeter as to be used by the French Navy. From that country we got our first artificial butter about 1873.

Italy as well as France secretly bought cotton oil to mix with olive mash, making a "pure olive oil" which was consumed all over the world.

Through a campaign of advertising its virtues, more and more Americans were induced to try it, until by 1880, the industry was firmly established, and cotton farmers began to pick up easy money for waste that their law had formerly prohibited them from dumping in a creek. About 182,000 tons were crushed that season; now 550 mills are consuming millions of tons.

Once the ball started, it rolled up an astounding variety of articles that were manufactured from cottonseed. The movie star who smears her face with ultra-expensive cosmetics, specially concocted in Paris, does not dream that its basis is our humble cottonseed. A farmer lad wounded at Belleau Wood, never imagines that the high explosive that hurt him is a cellulose product derived from cotton linters grown on daddy's farm.

Cottonseed makes paint for a tin roof and paint for my lady's cheeks. It makes collars for a horse and cushions for an automobile. The perfect lover wears a felt hat moulded from linters, while Sweetie's rayon dress is of the same material. Cottonseed provides salad oil for the connoisseur, and a cud for the cow.

On ante-bellum plantations pigs and cattle died from eating too much, but when dairy dietitians removed the deadly gossypol ingredient, then fed cottonseed meal mixed in proper proportions as a balanced ration, it proved to be the richest of all protein foods. Hulls are ground up and utilized as roughage for cattle.

In the light of a human delicacy, however, cotton

oil encountered a desperate opposition from dairy products. Cow men united with hog packers to fight, for in millions of kitchens today vegetable oils have almost driven out animal fats. The story runs —maybe it's not true—that fifty years ago at the Baltimore Grocers' Exchange, a group of celebrated chemists were employed to report cottonseed as unfit for human consumption. On the contrary, after every scientific test, they pronounced it superior in all respects to hog lard for cooking purposes, cleaner, did not become rancid, was more nutritious, more healthful, free from odor, and cheaper in the proportion of seven to twelve.

Far greater quantities would now be used by housewives were it not for state as well as federal laws that give preference to butter and lard. A tax of 15 cents on oleomargarine compels many poor families to eat rancid butter when they might use sweet vegetable oils.

From its multitudinous uses, the formerly worthless seed rose in value until oil alone is now estimated at one hundred and fifty million dollars, while seed products of all kinds total near a billion.

What this manna from heaven means to the farmer is incalculable, because seed at a fair average rate of $40 per ton gives him about $20 extra on every bale. Ginners usually buy it, and a sign board at the roadside announces their daily price.

In phenomenal seasons like 1918 and 1919, prime seed were scarce, and values rocketed to $84, even as high as $90 per ton. At $90 the farmer received $45 out of each bale for his seed, as much as he could realize for the lint itself at 9 cents a pound. This extra cash, as compared with fifty years ago, is pure velvet. Like getting money from home.

Seed money represents cash on the barrel head, and goes direct to the man that needs it most, the tenant. No matter if Wash Johnson be head over heels in debt and has no hope of paying his land-lord for rent or rations, nevertheless by a sort of plantation law the seed belong to Wash.

Black men are not Reds, neither Communists nor agitators, and rarely complain, yet a few dollars from their seed help mightily to keep them con-tented.

So when Wash drives his wagon of new-picked cotton to the gin, he yells out, "Run here, Mister Ginner. Run quick, an' gin de white folks' cotton off o' dis nigger's seed."

XIX

LO, THE POOR CROPPER

"YASSUH, boss," the old negro answered cheerfully, "I'se workin' twenty acres o' land for Mister Johnny, on de halves. Half an' half, suh; half an' half."

"Did you make a big crop?"

"Tol'able, suh, tol'able. De most I could do was jest to make Mister Johnny's half."

"The share cropper," says a wise man of our delta, "is a laborer who in fat seasons gets half the crop. In lean seasons he gets it all, sometimes more."

Each of these opposing viewpoints has its grain of truth, and so much has lately been printed in American newspapers it seems fair to tell what various people think. Irreconcilable statements are made and, true or untrue, form part of public opinion. This chapter does not attempt a scholarly analysis of causes or suggest a remedy, but merely gives what any observer must see and hear in our Cotton Belt.

Mr. David Cohn, of Greenville, Mississippi, in his excellent book, *God Shakes Creation,* speaks of hearing and seeing the same things. So does Mr. Lev Flournoy, staff writer for the Scripps-Howard

Newspapers, who investigated the so-called "Share Croppers War" in Arkansas. With grateful thanks to both these gentlemen some of their ideas are adopted.

The share cropper seems an institution peculiar to southern fields and was not maliciously devised for the purpose of exploiting a downtrodden class. As a forced arrangement it grew out of the Civil War, "jest growed," like Topsy, from necessity and poverty that followed defeat. Neither the planter nor the toilers, mostly black, who became share hands, could help themselves. There was nothing else to do except employ their sole asset to feed their families. The ex-Confederate landlord owned his acres, while the ex-slave, hungry and disillusioned, who drifted back to a ruined plantation, owned his muscle. Side by side they went to work.

The negro pauper was able to provide nothing, so the planter as best he might got hold of a mule or two, patched up his farm implements and scrapped around for rations until cotton was sold in September.

Today the share hand—let us say a negro, because we have so many more blacks than whites—goes to the boss in January inquiring for land. He has a wife and two small children; not a nickel, not a mule, cow or pig, but three dogs. To secure this labor the planter makes a considerable investment, cabin, land, mule, gear, tools, wagon, seed, amounting to above $2000. In addition he supplies the cropper with rations and other necessities on credit.

It is probably true that nowhere else on earth can an unskilled laborer cinch a living to himself and family for nine months ahead without having to worry about sickness, losing his job, or failing to eat three meals per day. Nobody except a cotton planter will make such contracts, certainly not the wheat grower of Dakota, or level-headed corn farmer in Illinois. If a wanderer off the highway should straggle in to rent some land, the Illinois or Dakota landlord requires references, and asks, "What equipment have you?"

"None."

"You can't farm without equipment. Good-by."

Consider the past season, a highly prosperous one in this section. Suppose the cropper cultivates twenty acres in cotton and at Christmas has picked out maybe fifteen bales. Fifteen bales are worth just about one thousand dollars, to be split fifty-fifty. On some plantations the cropper gets all the seed, and seed from fifteen bales bring him about $300 cash. Seed money is supposed to carry the cropper's family through the winter after his landlord stops issuing rations.

Out of his gross return the cropper pays his commissary account, also his pro rata of ginning, and for extra pickers if any were hired.

On this commissary account, or on money advanced to buy medicines, and unforeseen luxuries like a lawyer to get the cropper out of jail, the planter charges interest, sometimes as high as twenty per cent. This practice is denounced by some people as an outrage and robbery of the poor cropper. The planter, however, is taking long chances and has no security except a hope rather than faith that his share hand will stay on the property and gather the crop. Often the cropper doesn't stay. If drouth parches his field or weevils sting the bolls, in July he may see that he won't make enough cotton to pay for his rations, so the cropper "takes up" everything he can wheedle out of his landlord; then one evening the riding boss may notice him at work, but next morning his cabin door stands open and reveals its vacancy. His few sticks of furniture have been moved out during the night and the share hand is gone.

Losses of this sort, as the planter claims, justify him in charging high interest so as to break even on such transactions as a whole. The planter advances money that he himself has borrowed, of course at a smaller rate, and is hog-tied by a mortgage. He must pay, pay the last dollar, and cannot do it unless he protects himself against losses through indolence and irresponsibility. All losses fall on him in this one-sided partnership where the cropper has nothing to lose, but may stick both hands in his empty pockets and stroll away from a hopeless proposition, after he and his family have lived for six months at the planter's expense.

The above guess at a share hand's earnings may

hold true only in a season of good yield and high prices. Such years, however, do come to the delta, seasons when it has actually happened that a planter distributes among his croppers enough cash to buy the property and make each share hand an independent landlord.

It is not meant to give the impression that every cropper wallows in wealth every Christmas. They don't. North Carolina figures for 1932-33 show that 61.7 per cent of them broke even; 25 per cent went into the hole, while 9.4 per cent made money. It might be illuminating to know if more than 60 per cent of American railroads broke even in 1932-33. Did only 25 per cent of our merchants go into the hole? Did 9.4 per cent of the steel industry make money, and what of our banks?

When cotton values soar, the price of used cars will also go rocketing to the sky. Every cropper wants one, must have one. In a certain Mississippi town, to the left of a bridge as you enter, there was once an open half-acre packed with all makes of automobiles. That space now stands empty, not a car on the lot, one hundred and fifteen being sold by a single dealer in a single week, mostly to delta negroes who paid from forty to four hundred dollars cash.

Outsiders who know nothing of share croppers, white, black, or yellow, might imagine that a man of that oppressed class, with $400 cash, would buy a mule, gear and implements, so that next season

he'd be a renter and get three-quarters instead of
half the crop. Will Wash Johnson do that? Watch
the roads and see Wash drive into a filling station
with a ten-cent cigar cocked upward in his mouth.
"Fill her full, boss," he shouts. "Fill her plum
full. I loves to ride." He buys sardines, striped
candy, bananas; skins off a twenty from his roll
to pay for repairs; chases women; drinks whisky,
smashes his car, and walks home dead broke.

By the first of February, Wash Johnson stands
just where he stood twelve months ago, across the
counter from a commissary clerk, drawing rations
on the credit of next year's crop.

Planters frequently waste their breath pleading
with a favorite negro, as former Governor John M.
Parker of Louisiana did when old Jake had nine
hundred dollars due him at the end of the season.
Parker called the greybeard patriarch aside and
said, "Jake, you made a pile of money."

"Sho did, Mister John. Me an' de boys done
tol'able good, suh. Tol'able good."

"Now, listen. Let me invest it for you. Buy a
piece of land so you won't have rent to pay, and—"

No use. At the end of their argument old Jake
still stood by his original gun; he craved to hear
that money rattle in his jeans, didn't want checks,
didn't want currency, just nine hundred silver dollars, all silver, to make a pleasing jingle as he
strutted.

He got the cash, then with dressed-up wife and

boys Jake departed hence, leaving Alsatia Plantation for a splurge of joy.

A week later Governor Parker received a telegram from the Chief of Police at Memphis asking if he would guarantee a return deck passage on the steamboat for Jake and his stranded family. The radiant negroes came home, bringing a bass drum, a banjo, and several toot horns, all that was left to show for a year of hard work.

White share croppers are often just as lazy, just as improvident as the blacks. A white woman of that stripe, sunk-jawed, freckled, with hair the color of dead straw, went to a social worker and told of four starving children and a sick husband. That part of her tale proved true; the family lived in wretched squalor and the social worker issued an order for groceries several weeks in succession. The destitute woman, however, didn't buy groceries but sneaked around to an unscrupulous merchant who slipped her a bit of cash, then the slab-sided vamp lolled back in a chair at Madame Beulah's Beauty Shoppe while the attendant adorned her with a permanent wave.

What are you going to do about it?

Among the share croppers are many excellent people, right feeling, religious, kind, but lacking those qualities that accumulate property or command success. At industrial centers this class holds the lowest-paid positions, last to be hired in boom years, and first to be fired when business gets slack.

In our Cotton Belt the same kind of people become share croppers.

Plantation cabins often seem unfit to stable a self-respecting mule, but are now being improved without help or encouragement from their occupants. At their worst, living conditions of share croppers are more sanitary and healthful than those of many industrial workers who are crowded in the slums of our richest cities.

The average tenant or cropper takes no care of his landlord's property, and never thinks to shove a shingle in a leaky roof to keep the rain from his own bed. In winter he won't exert himself to go to the woods and fetch fuel for his fire, but burns the pickets from his fence or pulls up flooring from the front porch. Once in a while some theoretical planter takes a pride in building model cabins, with paint, flowers and beautification. He screens their houses to protect tenants from malarial mosquitoes, then discovers that they punch great holes in front door screens so dogs can get in; and other holes in kitchen windows for convenience in throwing out slop.

If a cabin catches fire, a tiny blaze that might easily be extinguished, the cropper simply tosses out his own belongings and lets the white folks' property burn. He won't suffer because the boss must provide other quarters or lose the crop. That's that.

On some plantations it is deplorably true that both croppers and tenants have been exploited. This age-old wrong is not confined to cotton, or to white men who impose on blacks. Since the birth of time ignorant and helpless creatures have been preyed upon by the strong and crafty. On settlement day it's easy for the avaricious white man to out-figure an ignorant black who cannot read, and whether he cheats him or not, the negro usually believes it. Better-class planters always pay their croppers to the last cent, yet by a queer kink of negro nature, they show no more loyalty and work no harder for a square landlord than they will for those who swindle them, oftentimes not as hard.

This phase of the tangle is passing, partly because the negro is more intelligent, and partly because of an aroused public opinion among the whites.

For upwards of seventy years the cropper system has rocked along while nobody did anything more than grumble until two young men got together at an Arkansas village where they drew up a declaration which asserted the rights of agricultural labor and demanded redress. Opinions vary, profoundly and profanely vary, as to these two young men and their motives, some applauders hailing them as apostles of a new freedom, while scoffers contend that the whole stink was stirred up by imported Communists to make trouble, and at the same time to make money from dues and raking in philanthropic contributions.

Be that as it may, one pants presser and one filling station operator, neither of them apparently having any connection with agriculture, did organize the

Southern Tenant Farmers' Union, at Sunnyside
School House in eastern Arkansas across the river
from Memphis. Whatever their private aims, al-
truistic or financial, one pants presser and one filling station operator started something that made
front page stuff for American newspapers. Through
this organization and at mass meetings, croppers demanded one dollar per day for field labor, and protested against being "robbed" by landlords. Landlords hotly denied any robbery, and insisted that the
share hand's poverty was due to the fact that he
worked less than four months in a year and refused
to help feed himself. That he loafed through eight
long idle months, then expected to run an automobile, which no indolent peasant can do anywhere
in the world.

There was plenty of talk, both wild and conservative. One planter in the neighborhood tells of two
families whose men were prominently connected
with the crusade. They came on his plantation and
asked to pick cotton. He assigned them to cabins
where they and their families lived for fourteen
months, but declined to hit a lick of work. They
didn't pick one single lock of cotton or scratch the
ground with a hoe, did absolutely nothing except
make trouble for some day hands whom the planter
had set to plowing near their houses. Being settled
on his property the planter couldn't get rid of them
for more than a year, until finally and legally he
had the sheriff evict both families.

Newspapers carried sensational stories of meetings being broken up, of mobs and whippings. Two men were killed, others disappeared. And we heard through the public press of a Union official being sought by the Federal government for using the mails to defraud.

It is difficult to get at the underground truth, and we give much of this as rumor that shows an inflamed local sentiment which reached the state capitol at Little Rock. Governor Futrell called a conference of merchants, planters, bankers to meet with croppers and their champions in a free-for-all discussion.

Mr. Lev Flournoy in one of his Scripps-Howard articles says that the Union was not of Communists. "What gave them the Communistic odor was the fact that every Communist whose committee could afford railroad fare sent him into northeast Arkansas and financed him in persistent meddling."

On their part an officer of the Union announces the gradual weeding out of all Communists, "who volunteered their help and came near spoiling the show by prejudicing neutral observers."

Anyhow the pants presser and filling station operator caused a mighty commotion which was taken up by various "Leagues" and "Alliances" in other parts of the United States. We'll see what we see.

The Resettlement Administration of Arkansas, Louisiana and Mississippi has already found homes for 11,000 families on small farms supervised and financed by the government, with an ultimate aim of cooperative communities in cotton and food stuffs. How far this project may succeed no clairvoyant can guess, because it depends on what industry, thrift, and intelligence—or the opposite—the croppers themselves will bring to the experiment.

Long observation in our delta leaves one with the feeling that its evils are not altogether evils of a system, but may be more chargeable to the laxity of human nature. Hundreds if not thousands of Italian farmers have emigrated to this section without a cent, to start as share hands or tenants, worked a few years, spent no money, and gone home comparatively rich, while natives white and black remain as share hands.

If by some miracle our croppers should suddenly become industrious and look ahead, they soon must own the country and the system be automatically abolished.

XX

EXPORTS

WASH JOHNSON can't eat his cotton, and wears mighty few rags of it himself in the good old summer time. Cotton is the only important farm product none of which the farmer uses at home until it is processed by somebody else. Very little corn, for example, travels farther than fifteen miles from the patch on which it sprouted, while cotton may commute half-way around the globe before returning to Wash in the shape of an all-wool overcoat.

A commonplace bale as it stands on the gin platform could not be suspected of concealing such wanderlust proclivities anymore than a square-built housewife might conceal a secret passion for the sea. Yet cotton is a chronic gypsy. More than 50 per cent of the world crop goes rambling along trade routes, and aliens fashion it into new shapes. From the factories of white men, yellow men and little brown men, the finished product scatters, sending a fathom of cloth to the naked African, high explosives that thunder on the battleships, or a gauzy fabric to reveal the loveliness of some Parisian cocotte.

It has been only a few years since the easy-going

world rocked along serenely and 60 per cent of Wash Johnson's crop went over seas, bringing back a steady flow of gold that gave life to every American enterprise. Cotton money is not local, but national, and so important that our banks could not finance a copper mine in Arizona or a new railroad in Alaska if its returning stream were suddenly shut off. Credits would tighten, loans be difficult, and without cotton exports no prophet is now wise enough to foresee how the South might exist.

Not the southerner alone, but all Americans must feel a deep concern, concern and alarm at seeing foreign consumption dwindle until we now supply 45 per cent of world needs instead of 60 per cent.

Some of our lost trade may be accounted for by the fact that American long staple, celebrated among the spinners of fine goods, was practically abandoned when the boll weevil invaded our fields. That variety of fibre requires more time to mature, and the hungry pest ate it up.

Most of the material for this chapter is taken from statistical tabulations, and speeches or printed articles of big operators who oppose what is called our "American Cotton Policy." Opponents are far more vocal than defenders. Defenders seem to sit steady in the boat and keep their mouths shut, while attackers present an array of figures and arguments.

We do not mean to slur the cotton exchanges that make honest efforts to give, and do give out accurate information. Neither is it intended to discredit world merchants who sell our product to all the nations of the earth. Nevertheless the jingle of the guinea does influence human judgment, and it is well enough to know.

Before Eli Whitney sat at Mrs. Greene's fireside brooding over a machine to separate lint from seed, cotton fabrics were robes of royalty, too rich for a poor man's blood. Only 5 per cent of human garments were made of cotton. A sudden cheapness, however, extended its uses until 75 per cent to 80 per cent of mankind now wear this universal fabric. Prodigious demands stimulated the clearing of new fields, and the whir of more spindles at manufacturing centers.

Of all lands on earth our Southern Cotton Belt was best suited to the staple. We have the most fertile soil, a nearly ideal distribution of rainfall, and the essential labor. Because of natural advantages the South at once assumed and held its leadership, for half a century producing 60 per cent to 65 per cent as against the rest of the combined world.

Some, not much, of our staple was then spun at home by mills in New England states, leaving the bulk of the crop to British spinners. Europe, with hordes of textile workers, cannot grow its own raw material. After the Civil War, Liverpool continued to be the South's best customer; next came Le Havre, then New York and Boston. British spindles during that period accounted for about 70 per cent of our entire exports.

Since the World War, however, Lancashire mills have languished, while those in Japan sprang into aggressive life. In 1928-9 the Mikado's Empire exported less than half the yardage of cotton cloth that was sent out by England. But British trade declined while Japan's improved, until in 1933 Japanese exports had become almost equal, running neck and neck. Today Japan buys more raw cotton from us than anybody else, with Germany second, and Great Britain third. England now spins about three million bales annually, buying a million and a half from the United States. When the World War broke out, British spindles consumed just about twice that much.

To offset our loss of British trade, Japan imports three times as much cotton as she did twenty-five years ago, mixing American staple with shorter stuff from India. Bremen is the largest importer on the Continent, and Barcelona, Spain, took 300,000 American bales every year until civil war broke out.

These, with smaller purchasers here and there, constitute the principal sources of American cotton money that maintains the balance of world trade in our favor, so it is no joke when customers are weaned away.

Take this concrete example: during 1933 England imported one and a half million American bales as against thirty thousand from Brazil. Next year, 1934, her American purchases dropped to 910,000 bales, while British spinners bought 378,000 of Brazilian staple.

Apropos of which the *Manchester* (England) *Guardian* remarks, "The big decline in American imports has been due almost entirely to the scarcity and dearness of southern offers, resulting from the large amount of cotton withheld against the Washington 12 cent loans to farmers. This policy of artificially raising the price of American cotton has encouraged spinners to take cheaper outside cotton —particularly Brazilian and Indian.—"

International merchants, like Mr. Clayton and Mr. McFadden, insist that the falling off of American sales abroad is not due to lack of world buying power, or lesser consumption. As a matter of fact mankind is using much more cotton today than was consumed in prosperous times following the World War. A new record for high consumption is now being set. Yet, while cotton exports dropped so that for every American bale sold our competitors sold two, at that same time (1934) foreigners bought more than double the amount of our automobiles both in volume and in value.

The world has money to buy more tobacco from us, more industrial machinery, more trucks, iron and steel, but has substituted foreign cotton for ours.

The tariff—again quoting big operators—is largely to blame for this calamity. The whole world now owes Uncle Sam. He is the universal creditor, and cotton must be paid for by goods that he imports from other nations who can't climb over his tariff wall. Tariff arguments, pro and con, have been so exhaustibly thrashed out that we merely mention them.

Another factor is the growth throughout the world of a nationalistic spirit to "Buy at Home." Rates of exchange on money also affect the market. These are minor matters, however, according to world traders who contend that the chief cause of declining exports is our "American Cotton Policy" which stimulates competition by prices 20 per cent higher than foreigners could have realized except for our "pegging system." Taken altogether, a number of combined causes have lost our foreign markets for three and a half million bales annually. Most of this loss, say the traders, is traceable directly to a policy that has priced American cotton out of the market.

Part of our foreign loss is made up at home, more than one-third of the American crop now being consumed by spindles almost on the fields that produce it. Better highways through the southeastern states enable growers to truck their fibre direct to mills for distances as great as two hundred and fifty miles, which saves the cost of compressing and railroad charges.

Farmers west of the Mississippi River are hardest hit by loss of exports, because Texas and Oklahoma have practically no spindles, but depend on bales that go down to the sea in ships. Before 1915 cot-

AMERICAN COTTON DESTINED FOR THE MARKETS OF THE WORLD

ton production east of the Mississippi exceeded that on the west. With settlers pouring into Oklahoma and Texas, the balance has so shifted that Texas now produces more cotton than any other political subdivision of the earth. And Texas *must* sell her cotton abroad, 90 per cent of it.

XXI

FOR AND AGAINST THE COOPERATIVES

WHILE a one-gallus farmer wrestles with his plow in the hot sun, he gets mightily pestered to see a city slicker sit in the shade and figure him out of fat profits on his cotton. The hand is quicker than the eye, and bewildered farmers didn't see how the trick was turned, but values disappeared in some mysterious manner like the rabbit from a magician's hat.

Producers claim that there's too much waste, too high charges by ginners, warehousemen, railroads, middlemen. Often, they complain, a buyer will clear $25 on a single bale which is more profit than its producer can make on that same bale.

The "spread" is too great. "Spread" signifies this: the spinner pays $75 for a bale of cotton, but the $75 does not reach the farmer; a deduction here, a commission there, a profit yonder is subtracted, so that when his money filters back from New York the farmer counts $50 instead of $75.

One abuse that doesn't amount to much on any single bale illustrates a multitude of other petty wastes. It is called the "City Crop," because it grows on the floor of city warehouses where cotton is stored and samples taken. Handsful of lint are

snatched out, pulled over, examined and dropped
as "loose" to become the perquisite of some fellow
who hasn't spent one drop of sweat in its production.
The "City Crop" runs into considerable figures.
Everybody who looks at a bale of cotton gets his
rakeoff, so the farmer is in worse fix than a guest
who leaves a European hotel to run the gauntlet of
waiters, chambermaids, porters, bellhops and cab-
bies with greedy hands outstretched demanding tips.

From the farmer's point of view as his cotton
travels north along the road from field to mill, and
cash proceeds travel south, various nibblers pinch
his profits. The gears must be wrong, and farmers
talked about "orderly marketing" instead of "dumping." By "dumping" he means that too much of
his crop is rushed to market as soon as ginned, and
he can't help himself because he owes the merchant
for supplies, the merchant owes the bank for cash
to finance dozens of farmers, while the local financier
has strained his credit to secure funds from New
York. When times get tight in September, the City
Croesus shuts down on his country correspondent,
the country bank crowds the merchant, and the merchant who holds a mortgage on the farmer's crop
forces him to sell.

This is not tyrannical or wantonly oppressive, but
merely a condition under which the farmer cannot
act as a free agent, or hold his crop for better prices.
Therefore cotton is dumped on the market. Farmers
believe that dumping breaks the price, that values

mount again after he sells his crop and middlemen get rich.

Cotton statisticians, however, insist and exhibit figures over a course of years to prove that dumping does not appreciably lower prices.

To minimize the dumping evil, real or apparent, farmers caught up the slogan of "orderly marketing," which has a pleasing tinkle in the ear. Just a tinkle as many people claim. The idea was that one-twelfth of the crop should be sold each month as consumers were able to absorb it.

Individual farmers could do nothing to correct certain practices that they believed were eating them alive, which led to organization under the Capper-Volstead Act of 1922 when cooperative cotton associations were authorized by law as mutual benefit societies, composed solely of producing farmers who pooled their crops for collective sale, supposedly sharing profits and bearing losses.

For seven years cooperatives rocked along satisfactorily in a small way—or staggered along, according to who tells it—without "government subsidies" until 1929. The facts should be definitely ascertainable, yet we find irreconcilable differences in assertions.

Critics of cooperatives insist that they have lost some hundred and forty millions of public money and are hopelessly bankrupt unless the United States will save them. Contra, the cooperatives stoutly maintain that losses incurred by the Federal Farm

Board should not be charged against them, when $1,700,000 of their honestly accumulated capital was confiscated from them to help make good a deficit created by the Federal Farm Board for which co-operatives were not responsible.

Cooperative officials point to page and paragraph of the record, and insist that the Farm Board, organized under President Hoover, designated them as agents to carry out the 16-cent loan on cotton. That cooperatives didn't make the law, didn't decide how much money should be advanced or to whom; that they obeyed orders from higher-up and exercised no discretion whatever. They were chosen for this service because of agencies throughout the Cotton Belt, and direct contacts with farmers.

It was not a profit-making device, the agreement being that cooperatives should be reimbursed for expenses incurred, costs, salaries and overhead.

At the time of these loans cotton sold at 18 cents but dropped to such a figure that the government lost millions by no fault of the co-ops. Then, in final settlement, the Attorney General of the United States ruled that, under existing statutes, the co-ops could not be reimbursed for certain overhead expenses and carrying charges. So their own reserves, money that belonged to American farmers, were taken to patch up a gap. The matter is still being discussed, still a bone of contention.

For one reason and another—chiefly one—a powerful opposition to cooperatives crystallized in U. S.

Senate Resolution No. 185, under which their methods were investigated at Memphis, beginning October 28th, 1935.

Eighty-odd witnesses were interrogated. As part of his testimony the Honorable Norris C. Williamson, President of the American Cooperatives, introduced letters to show that merchants and exchanges had been active and spent money to procure the attendance of hostile witnesses. Yet only twenty farmers made statements of grievance or complaint against the cooperatives—twenty out of a membership that totals 260,000. Senator Bankhead, one of the Investigating Committee, subsequently emphasized this fact.

Mr. Williamson, former State Senator, has long been recognized as a leader in Louisiana, owning and successfully managing plantations near Lake Providence. Much of this chapter is prepared from material given by him and naturally favorable to cooperatives.

Trade antagonism, as he conceives, is due to the fact that for fourteen years cooperative competition has forced cotton merchants to pay all farmers, whether members or not, more nearly the value of their products.

Before the cooperatives began distributing accurate price information, farmers found themselves paying tribute to the tune of from $5 to $25 per bale to merchants, because when they sold their cotton they didn't know what it was worth. Often they sold a crop "hog round," the merchant paying, say, 10 cents per pound "all around" for a hundred bales of various grade and staple. Then the merchant would cull out finer staples worth maybe a few cents more, and get his profit from the premium. As long as farmers were prosperous and received a high price they didn't realize how much went into the "kitty" and had plenty of money to spend anyhow. But when values dropped so low they could not meet obligations for crop loans, were unable to pay taxes, had to withdraw their boys and girls from college and put them to work, then they commenced to look around and locate the trouble. Deeper thought suggested that there ought to be some method of getting the consumer's dollar for their cotton. Possibly by pooling their products and selling directly to spinners they might save many charges of middlemen. That's exactly what our cooperative movement means. Attacks on cooperatives are simply attacks on the right of farmers to sell direct to consumers.

The movement started by an organization of staple growers in 1922, Mississippi and Oklahoma being the first. Next year other states followed. Since that time, according to studies made by the U. S. Department of Agriculture, and by agricultural colleges in the South, the "spread" between the price received by farmers and the price paid by spinning mills has been reduced to about $1 per bale, instead of $5 to $25 per bale, depending upon the quality of the cotton and length of staple.

Wider "spreads" were formerly common on long staple, because farmers didn't know their real value and the cotton merchant did know. Many a farmer who has raised cotton all his life knows little or nothing about its staple which has now reached the fine point of being measured in thirty-seconds of an inch. The expert classer for a merchant sees at once that out of several bales offered by the farmer, two of them are five-thirty-seconds instead of an eighth, consequently worth more money. But he doesn't pay more unless a classer for the cooperatives puts the farmer wise.

The cotton merchant naturally wants to cinch a profit, buying his cotton as cheap as he can, and selling as high as he can. Cooperative associations have only one purpose, to sell a member's cotton at the best figure. Savings from the "spread" go into the farmer's pocket, while the merchant's profits swell his own purse.

Farmers through their cooperatives now sell collectively about 12 per cent of our American crop, while merchants quarrel because they have only 88 per cent left. This 12 per cent, however, is not the reason, it's the price that merchants must pay on the 88 per cent because cooperatives keep the farmer posted. Every agency in the Cotton Belt receives daily quotations of "base price" on grades and staple. Any farmer, member or non-member, may get correct quotations, and the cooperatives will pay that much money for one bale or a hundred thousand. So if merchants buy cotton at all they must give the producer at least what he can get through his own organization.

That's where his shoe pinches the cotton merchant and makes him holler. It is no longer possible, if our facilities are used, for staple to be snapped up at less than market value.

Cooperatives do not buy "hog round" but appraise each bale separately, then assemble them in even-running lots and sell to spinners. Opponents claim that producers are allowed no better prices by cooperatives than other merchants pay, which is possibly true sometimes, because it might happen that a buyer to fill a hurry order for the mill, may concede a few points.

Remember, however, that but for our active competition and the information we furnish farmers, merchants would buy cotton much cheaper.

Other valuable services rendered were in the lowering of freight rates, warehouses charges and insurance. For example, railroads actually carried glassware to New Orleans for less money, pound for pound, than they hauled a bale of cotton. From a certain town in Louisiana their rate was 78 cents per hundred, or $3.90 per bale. To fight that overcharge we trucked our cotton to the river and loaded it on barges at a cost of $1.50 per bale to New Orleans, until railroads had to meet that price or lose the hauling. Savings like this go directly to the farmer.

At present more than 260,000 cotton producers are bona fide members of different cooperatives. They pay reserves into their associations to build up capital structure for both state and national institutions. Professional cotton traders and other adversaries object to our method of securing membership, claiming that we have no genuine members, but farmers who own this organization are entirely satisfied.

It is asserted that we are subsidized and use government funds. As a matter of fact cooperatives do borrow money, but never exceeding 20 per cent of what is necessary to market their cotton. Additional funds we secure from commercial banks, principally in New York City, at a little above one-half of the rate of interest we pay to the Farm Credit Administration. We pay 1-11/16 per cent to New York banks, about the same as is charged to any large commercial enterprise, while to the U. S. Farm Credit Administration we pay 3 per cent.

Since the American Cotton Cooperative Association was organized, this Government has not lost one cent, not one single penny on any loan advanced for their operations. The statement that cooperatives lost millions of dollars in 1931 refers to the Federal Farm Board and its attempt to stabilize a 16-cent loan as we have previously pointed out.

Ultimate losses sustained by the Government represented the difference between money advanced to farmers and amounts ralized from their cotton when finally sold.

In the McKellar hearing at Memphis, Mr. James C. Stone, President of the Federal Farm Board, testified that this adjustment was unfair to cooperatives who should be reimbursed for that loss. Senator Smith of South Carolina also stated before an investigating committee:

"I maintain here and now, in justice to the Cooperatives, that the Government, or the Farm Board set up by the Government, was morally and financially bound to shoulder any loss incident to the decline of cotton below 16 cents.—The fact remains that Cooperatives were asked to be the channel through which the Farm Board could approach the producer and get his cotton; therefore they were morally and financially bound to make good.— When defeat came the Government should have accepted it in good faith and put these people [the cooperatives] right back where they found them.— Restitution ought to be made."

U. S. Senator Kenneth McKellar of Tennessee who led the fight on cooperatives at Memphis, announced views directly contrary to those of Mr. Williamson.

In a debate on the floor of the Senate, Senator McKellar said:

"I have no objection to cooperatives as cooperatives. I am thoroughly for any cooperative that will be a benefit to the farmers; but the American Cotton Cooperative Association is not a cooperative association at all. It is simply and solely a cotton merchant, just as Anderson-Clayton & Co. or McFadden & Co. The only difference is that the A.C.C.A. is subsidized by our federal government while the others are not subsidized.

"—These cooperatives were authorized under the law of 1922 and until 1929 were without substantial government subsidy. In 1929 a revolving fund of $500,000,000.00 was established for the purpose of aiding farmers through cooperatives. The A.C.C.A. started out with an authorized capital of $30,000,-000.00 of which $800,000.00 was subscribed, and $76,950.00 paid in. $40,600.00 was afterward returned to marketing associations, so that the actual capital of the concern in real money was $30,350.00. With this scanty backing the A.C.C.A. deals in a million and a half bales of cotton, because it has been subsidized by the government in almost unlimited measure.—

"First the 'Farm Board Subsidy,' and the A.C.C.A. lost out of that the small amount of $79,-286,384.00, nearly $80,000,000.00 lost principally in speculation, and it has been speculating ever since.—

"It has no members except its own officers and agents, servants of various subsidiaries. The only members it could claim were obtained in this way: Assume that I am a cotton farmer and the gentleman from South Carolina (Senator Smith) represents the Cooperatives in my county. I sell him a bale of cotton just as if he were a merchant, and agree on the price, say, 10 cents per pound. He hands me a bill of sale, and in this bill of sale is a statement that by reason of his buying the cotton I become a member of the A.C.C.A. Maybe I am a colored man, or a poor white boy who cannot read. I make a mark. I have sold my cotton and wish to get the money but cannot get it unless I sign the statement agreeing that I am a member of the A.C.C.A.—

"Here's an instance of how it works: A colored farmer took one bale of cotton to the Mid-South Cotton Growers Association at Memphis and received for that bale $51.31. The Association had made him a previous advance of $5.59, charging him interest of 60¢, insurance $1.30, storage $4.55; other charges, and God knows what they were, amounted to $1.40. Then they deducted $5.00 membership fee. They were publishing a newspaper and he was debited with a subscription to that, 50¢, altogether a total of $19.34 taken out of that poor man's cotton money. If that is aid to farmers through Cooperatives, then God have mercy on the poor farmer.—

"The next farmer received $53.97 for his cotton,

deducting $5.00 membership, 50¢ newspaper and other charges amounting to $19.75.

"About a year ago the A.C.C.A. had difficulties over money. They had been borrowing from the Department of Agriculture at from one quarter of one per cent to one half of one per cent, and lending it out to farmers at 5½%. This statute was repealed and they were required to pay 3%.—

"Mr. Creekmore, their vice-president and general manager, went to New York and arranged with several banks to borrow at 1-11/16%, provided our government would subordinate its securities to the claim of the city bank. That's what happened. Our government actually subordinated its loan so that cooperatives might get money at 1-11/16% to lend the farmers at 5½%.

"Think of that. This enormous concern already subsidized to the extent of more than $140,000,-000.00.—

"A cotton cooperative is supposed to be an organization of cotton farmers for mutual benefit by means of which the profits are divided and the losses borne equally. I find from the testimony that profits are not divided equally or proportionately. They have not had any profits. Mr. Creekmore, President of this institution, testified that the A.C.C.A. would go into bankruptcy unless the government continued to lend. It had failed twice, and the government had twice paid it out."

Being asked on the Senate floor if members did not have a right to vote and elect officials, Mr. Mc-Kellar answered:

"Theoretically the members have a right to vote and control their affairs. Actually they do not vote and do not meet. I do not believe that a man could be found in the great cotton county of Shelby, Tenn., who would say that he was a member of the co-operatives or has ever attended one of their meetings. —There are no local organizations anywhere except in a few counties of Mississippi where they seem to have had an old organization in several counties, but nowhere else.—

"Prices paid by the A.C.C.A. to its so-called members are not higher than those paid by private merchants, and the cost of handling is greater. It is of no more value to the farmer than is Weil & Co., Mc-Fadden & Co., Anderson-Clayton & Co., or any other large cotton merchant."

Senator Townsend of Delaware appears to have taken no part in the actual investigation at Memphis, but signed the majority report, while Senator Bankhead of Alabama, third member of the committee, files a minority report:

"My approval is withheld from the report submitted by Senator McKellar. The following conclusions seem warranted by the testimony:

"The American Cotton Cooperative Association and its affiliates are farmer-owned and farmer-controlled, organized and operated in accordance with the letter and spirit of cooperative marketing laws.

"The record shows that in performing the ordinary functions of cooperative marketing associations, exclusive of stabilization operations, the American Cotton Cooperative Association and its affiliates on the whole have rendered satisfactory service. Out of over a quarter of a million producer members, less than twenty-five appeared [at Memphis] to protest any grievance or criticism.

"The evidence shows that cotton cooperatives lost certain reserves and were put in debt to the federal government as a direct result of stabilization efforts conducted under direction of our government acting through the Federal Farm Board. The record further disclosed that since the cessation of these stabilization activities by the government, the operation of the Cotton Cooperatives as a whole has been conducted in accordance with sound business and cooperative principles.

"The American Cotton Cooperative Association was organized in 1930 by thirteen state and regional associations with a paid-up capital of only $76,-950.00. This association has accumulated a substantial capital and surplus through earnings. At the close of the 1933-34 season their capital and surplus amounted to $2,355,658.59, and all of this except the original $76,950 was a result of earnings. These earnings are held for the benefit of producers whose patronage contributed to it. At the close of the 1933-34 season $480,058.20 was distributed by this association as patronage dividends. These results have been accomplished in spite of some testimony by the cotton trade to the effect that the American Cotton Cooperative Association and its affiliates were paying more to producers than the trade could afford to pay, and were selling cotton to the mills at lower prices than the trade could afford to take.

"I am compelled to the conclusion that during these years the cooperatives have reduced the spread between producer and consumer to the benefit of both.

"The record does not justify an assumption that capital loans to cooperatives are worthless, or that the government will ultimately lose thereby.

"The cooperatives have rendered noteworthy service. Through local offices and receiving agents, classing service is widely provided, to the end that farmers who do not know the grade or staple of their cotton may be advised.

"The public policy of the United States is committed to cooperative marketing, which is endorsed in the platform of both political parties.

"It is a fair deduction too that the cooperatives lost their reserve which they held for farmer members, as a direct result of stablization operations initiated by our federal government. The former chairman of the Federal Farm Board frankly stated that his board at the close of operations was compelled to make the harsh and unfair settlement with the cooperatives based upon a legal interpretation of existing statutes. I am forced to the conclusion that Congress, who alone can right the wrong, should by appropriate legislation restore to the cooperatives and their producer members, the reserves which were thus appropriated."

There's both sides of the case now pending before the U. S. Senate, in the words of Sir Lucius O'Trigger, "a very pretty quarrel as it stands."

XXII

EXPERIMENT STATIONS

" 'TAIN'T nary one o' them spectacled professors from Washington, Dee See, kin larn *me*
nothin'." This was a common remark some years
ago when stubborn farmers clomped hard on their
quids and shut their jaws like bear-traps as speakers
from the Department of Agriculture tried to make
them realize a desperate situation.

Boll weevil had already destroyed southeast Texas,
and though not one of them had yet crossed the
Sabine River into Louisiana, Department Entomologists foresaw the unpreventable infestation of our
entire Cotton Belt. Alarmed by the danger, earnest
agents went to every community trying to teach cotton farmers how to minimize the ravages that were
certain. They spoke at mass meetings in court
houses, schools, everywhere, distributed bulletins
and showed pictures to incredulous country people
who wouldn't believe, but scoffed and jeered at city
fellers that didn't know a darn thing about hoeing
or plowing. "Can't larn *me* nothin'! Can't larn *me*
nothin'. Huh! Makin' all that fuss about a bug."

Hard heads didn't learn a thing while the pest
moved steadily towards them forty miles a year,
forty miles, forty miles, yet the farmer who lived

forty-one miles away jogged along in the same rut until weevil ate him up. Only a few of them, even the more intelligent, heeded persistent warnings, but continued their slipshod planting of cotton, cotton, and took no precautions.

Stealthily by night, almost unnoticed by day, the pest marched eastward and the opening of each new season found Mrs. Weevil stinging bolls nearer to the Atlantic Ocean, the only barrier that might stop her. Behind her she left a swath of desolated farms and destitute farmers who learned nothing.

Outside the good old U. S. A. foreigners smile tolerantly at some of our national institutions but always take off their hats to the American Department of Agriculture. It is known the world over and respected for practical achievement and common sense.

Far in advance of anybody else, the Department foresaw what must happen, and what actually did happen. Their best men had long been posted at the Texas front, studying weevil in stricken fields, spying out their habits under microscopes and devising methods of control.

This insect, as well they knew, was not a temporary invader to swarm over the land like locusts, then vanish. Weevil had come and weevil would remain, a permanent enemy which could not be exterminated, so unless the South acknowledged itself whipped and abandoned cotton, we had to plan a campaign of defense to be successfully carried on year after year.

A fight to the death. Scientists from the Department based their battle on three fundamental ideas that interlocked, one supplementing the other. First: an offensive to diminish the weevils' numbers and prevent too rapid breeding. Second: better varieties of cotton that would mature and be gathered before the pest could destroy it. Third: intensive cultivation.

To these three cardinal points they added the same eternal preachment that had always fallen on deaf ears—cotton farmers must raise their own food stuffs for man and beast.

Everywhere throughout our Cotton Belt experts made the same determined effort which can be more clearly understood by confining ourselves to their work at one point, The Delta Experiment Station, Stoneville, Mississippi.

This competent organization operates under the United States Department of Agriculture, and so far as cotton is concerned deals chiefly with long strong fibre that grows on alluvial lands beside the Mississippi River. The excellence of these "benders" for the weaving of fine fabrics gave America its preeminence in cotton markets of the world; but when attacked by weevil they could no longer be produced. Not a chance. Because long staple requires more weeks to mature, and by that time myriad millions of weevil will eat it up. So our

delta cotton was doomed and the Department foresaw it years before the calamity befell.

Men massed their forces against the bug, and two
sets of experimenters went to work, one squad attempting to weaken the attack by poisoning and killing such of the enemy as could be reached; while another squad built up the power of cotton to resist
attack.

Calcium arsenate applied by airplanes or ground
machines, with constant plowing between the rows
to throw hot dirt over fallen larvae, might hold the
weevil in check until a crop could be rushed through
and picked.

To rush a crop we must have an early-maturing
plant, and by process of selection, season after season, in their own broad fields at Stoneville, experimenters marked those stalks that showed the first
bloom, stalks that formed the first boll, and produced the first lint. Precocious plants were jealously
tended and their seed preserved to sow next season
in rows four feet apart each way. Every individual
plant was minutely observed. Individual charts
were kept, day by day, as if that stalk of cotton were
a patient in a sanitorium. Plant surgeons knew
daily how each patient responded to temperature,
drouth, moisture; knew the hour of the first blossom; knew whether the plant was subject to or re-
sistant to other diseases. Experimenters watched
everything, chose the best plant for seed, and destroyed others. Eighty-five per cent of their selec-

tions were discarded because of some defect, and the same method carried forward with fifteen per cent that seemed more nearly perfect.

The process of selection and elimination required patience, ceaseless patience, never once letting a foot slip, or permitting a weaker strain to creep in. Results were definite and satisfactory, giving to the delta a dependable variety of cotton that matures its lint on an average of one month earlier than was ever known before. Thirty days at the close of a season makes a difference between crop success and crop failure.

However that's not all, only a part. While developing a quicker strain, experimenters did not lose sight of staple, but continually hybridized and pollenized the earliest plants so as to increase their length and strength of fibre, at the same time not delaying the hour when bolls burst open for the picker.

Patience, more patience; selection, more selection; generation bred unto generation, all with one purpose. Longer, finer, stronger staple was added, added, added to the best and quickest plants. Delta staple, however, is not yet what we had fifty years ago, when the plant might take all the time it needed to lengthen and strengthen its silky fibre. This, in some world markets, is spoken of as "deterioration of American cotton" which lessens its value in competition with foreign staple and decreases our exports. The Mississippi Delta cannot now offer to spinners a fibre that's quite the same.

Seed of annually improving earliness and staple were made available, and planters promptly took advantage of them. Farmers whose skulls still remained impervious, saw their neighbors, with seed from the experiment station, raising cotton in spite of the weevil, and began to change their minds.

After fixing the quick maturity of the plant and improving the staple, experimenters gave more attention to bolls. The cotton boll when it pops open like a chestnut bur, ordinarily contains four compartments called "locks," each lock holding its bit of lint. Here and there a plant showed up that had larger bolls with five locks, producing more cotton. Such plants were searched out, segregated, nursed and coddled to perpetuate a valuable propensity, and by interbreeding with early maturing long-staple varieties, the five-locked habits became established. Disease resistance was also watched, as a mother watches her babe in the cradle, and feeble strains cast aside.

By excellent teamwork the Bureau of Soils contributed to a common end, and planters soon realized the value of its service. On many farms there might appear a patch of ground where nothing would thrive. Cotton made a sorry show; no ears on the corn stalk; even the exuberant cowpea grew thin and scraggly. So the farmer sends a sample to the Experiment Station for analysis, and is told exactly what elements his soil requires.

Many a horny-handed farmer goes often to this station for advice. The place is wide open, no secrets; anybody can see anything at any time, and all questions answered.

Men who were fighting for their homes and fields had declared war on a bug and battled with every weapon of practical science.

How did the campaign end? It hasn't ended, it never will. The weevil, like the poor, is always with us.

Here's the present situation: Since 1922, 90 per cent of our Cotton Belt has been infested, the weevil emerging every spring from hibernation, and pessimists long ago predicted that southern fields must be given over to cockleburs. Very well, let us compare the yield before and after the pest began operation.

Half a century ago an acre of land east of the Mississippi River produced on an average 168 pounds of lint. Today from that same acre, under intensive cultivation and in spite of the weevil, the farmer picks 219 pounds of lint. At the close of 1931 they had gathered eighteen million bales, the biggest crop in human history.

Department experts have converted the scoffer and hushed his objections, so that dirt farmers no longer loaf around the store and jeer, "Them spectacled professors from Washington, Dee See, can't larn *me* nothin'."

XXIII

FOREIGN FIELDS

FARMERS who grow long staple in our alluvial country have always cast a jealous eye toward Egypt, an ancient land yet younger than we are in the production of cotton as a commercial crop.

Their triangular delta, with its three points at Cairo, Alexandria and Port Said, is twice as big as our Yazoo-Mississippi Delta, and its staple sells for higher prices.

Both these rival deltas drew their original fertility from the silt of a great river, which Egypt continues to do, year by year impounding the waters of the Nile and forcing the deposit of rich soil. At the same time the Egyptians irrigate their fields, for in the growing season that country has practically no rainfall.

Some wag once remarked that the Yazoo-Mississippi Delta was "cultivated by niggers and Kernels," meaning Wash Johnson and Colonel Woodville. So is Egypt. Aside from thousands of small land owners, princes of the Khedivial family hold large estates which are operated by pashas and fellaheen.

The agricultural laborer of the Nile is an Arab called a *fella*—plural *fellaheen*—chocolate-colored, bricky-brindle yellow, dusty looking as if he'd been sprinkled with ashes instead of talcum. The term *fella* designates a class, and has no reference to land ownership. Abdullah, the *fella,* may be lord of a thousand acres and heap up riches from cotton, yet in his native village he remains a *fella.*

At the beginning of each year a landless Abdullah goes to the agent of the Bey, who wears a red skull tarboosh which entitles him to be called *Effendi.* Abdullah, making certain mystic touches at his forehead, opens negotiations, "Upon you be peace and the blessings of Allah." The agent then inquires as to the health of Abdullah, who replies, "Praise be to Allah, I am in all good."

Perhaps Abdullah wants to pay a cash rent, so much a year per *feddan*—about an acre. A *feddan* may produce four hundred and fifty pounds of cotton; in good seasons six hundred pounds, worth nearly twice as much as American cotton.

For land that yields eighteen guineas' worth of staple, the *fella* agrees to a rent of fifteen guineas, or $75 per acre in American money. The princely owner of the land, Big Harem Bey, has much expense for ladies in Cairo and needs funds. Five-sixths to the Bey and one-sixth to the *fella,* is what makes such a difference between *fella* and Bey. In our Cotton Belt an acre that produces 400 pounds of lint, will rent for around $7.

In this country too the renter gets a house for himself and family to live in, free firewood, garden patch, and pasturage for his cattle. But when Abdullah takes five *feddan* he gets that much to the measured inch, no more, no less. Not a square foot to live on. He huddles at his village near by in a cluster of mud-and-dung huts, that resemble dirt daubers' nests. He doesn't get a single blade of grass for his goat, donkey or camel—if Abdullah be so prosperous as to own a camel. A good camel may cost ten guineas, enough to buy another wife, and an additional wife will produce additional sons to produce more cotton to buy more wives to produce more sons.

A negro tenant in the South can range the white folks' woods and catch possums, kill ducks or let his pigs get fat in the swamps, but Abdullah has the laugh on him in the matter of wives.

If Abdullah works on shares, he gets one-third and the landlord two-thirds of his crop. Again Wash Johnson has the long end of the bargain. It would seem that the Egyptian share hand receives a larger proportion than the *fella* who pays cash rent, but the rent-paying tenant also makes two other crops that have not yet been taken into account.

Abdullah does not get "furnish." Big Harem Bey cares nothing as to what the *fella* eats or where he sleeps. All he knows is "$75 per *feddan.*" So Abdullah squats in his own hut and munches a bit of *durra* bread, baked on a fire of dried camel's dung.

The *fella* wants but little here below and has two ways to get it. First he may go to the Greek. Anybody who wants anything in Egypt goes to the Greek, Monsieur Adonis Eleftheropolous.

Maybe Monsieur Adonis distrusts Abdullah for a bad risk, nevertheless takes a chance at big interest, ten or twelve per cent a year on the cash.

The Greek does not advance supplies. If Abdullah owned a *feddan* or two he'd have no trouble borrowing money on a simple note without security.

Should the Greek turn him down, Abdullah may go to the factor, with an oriental rigmarole at the end of which he says, "Oh, thou Effendi, I desire to sell you some cotton."

"How much?"

"Praise be to Allah, I shall sell you forty-five cantars. The crop is bad, very bad. Worms have gorged their bellies upon it and caterpillars eaten their fill. There is no cotton in all the land."

Up speaks the factor, "Go to, thou worker of miracles. By the beard of the prophet, how canst sell to me forty-five cantars if all the cotton has been destroyed?"

This fails to bluff Abdullah who comes to the bat again. "Oh, thou Effendi, the cotton of my neighbors and my friends has been destroyed. My own is good, most excellent Effendi. May Allah be bountiful to us all."

Between preliminaries and final frills, a bargain is struck. The *fella* sells his growing crop, or part of it, to the factor, who advances one guinea per cantar on cotton that Abdullah expects to gather.

Sometimes Abdullah pays interest and sometimes not.

Instead of haggling over a price at time of sale, Abdullah watches the quotations at Alexandria, so when he thinks that cotton is high enough, goes again to the factor and says, "I deliver my forty-five cantars as of this day at market price." This completes the transaction.

When a *fella* once enters upon land he never abandons it during that season. It does not follow, however, that he rents the same acres every year. He usually works in the same neighborhood and may rent from another landlord next year.

It sometimes happens that the population of one district is not sufficient to work the crops of that district, and laborers must be imported from less prosperous sections. The big Egyptian planter who needs more tenants does not hire a labor agent to corral them. He thinks of a village where crops are poor and which is overstocked with idlers. Then sends for their long-bearded sheik, Mustapha Ed-Din, with a stripe of green in his turban, marking said Mustapha as a descendant of the prophet. Thereupon sheik and planter traffic for a certain number of dingy Abdullahs which the sheik delivers according to contract, then hangs around to see that they work. Of course he gets his rakeoff.

Abdullah plants cotton in March and gets it off the land by September in order to sow wheat or other grain in October. Fodder for his stock he starts in January, then the ground is rested for six weeks until cotton time comes again.

Being a Mohammedan, he will not use imported machinery devised by the son of a Christian dog, but plows with a couple of humped-back bulls hitched to a long beam of wood, the end of which is shod with iron. He and his forefathers have plowed the same land in the same way for thousands of years, and far be it from Abdullah to shame his ancestors.

Allah sends down plenty of rain on our Mississippi Delta, while Abdullah toils mother naked in tiny irrigation ditches, bringing the elixir of life to each particular cotton plant. Water and not blood is the vital fluid of Egypt, so precious that nature can never afford to bathe her own face, and Abdullah dares not use it for other than irrigation purposes. Which is the obvious reason why nature and Abdullah both look so dingy.

Inundations of the Nile come with such clockwork regularity that the *fella* knows when to plant and when to harvest. It may be that Abdullah raises a few melons on a low island that stands uncovered except at high Nile. If the stranger inquires, "May not the river rise and overwhelm these fruits of thy labor?" Abdullah shakes his head and replies, "Allah is just, and harm cometh not to his servant. Floods will cover this land on *el talet,* the third day of the month *Ilool* at the down going of the sun."

If Mississippi planters could be so sure, they would not lose millions of dollars from overflow.

Through the slow-moving centuries Abdullah has been a water dipper. So many Abdullahs stand beside the Nile, dipping, dipping, dipping so persistently with *shadoof* and *sakieh;* so many women carry off the water in jugs, that they materially deplete the river's flow. We who live along the Mississippi could never imagine such phenomenon, but it's true.

Just before the last picking Abdullah sows grain or bersim between his cotton rows on land that's kept cleaner than an American gardener's seedbed. When the very last lock of cotton is gathered, he pulls up the stalk and carries it home, for Abdullah needs that stalk to feed his camel, donkey and goats.

Egypt may be old-timey in her tastes for tombs and pyramids, but is ages ahead of modern America when she markets her chief export. Stand on the dock at Liverpool and watch a cargo arrive from Pharaohland, neat trim bales, carefully covered and protected from damage, as if Egypt regarded her product as valuable. Then look at American cotton, ties burst off, bagging torn, and lint blowing all over the dock, like junk that's not worth wrapping up. All of which lowers the price to southern farmers, for spinners must reckon with the waste.

2

Owners of southern fields in new America are warned of another threat from a land that was already grey with age and producing cotton centuries before the Queen of Sheba went to keep her date with Solomon. British spinners are persistently pressing a development of the Sudan, and we might take a look at it.

South of Egypt from Wady Halfa to Khartum, miles of tawny river banks lie flat as a famished tiger with lips against the Nile, sucking greedily at a chocolate-colored water which is meat as well as drink. Limitless spaces glimmer in the sun, space, nothing but space, desolate space that like eternity has no beginning and no end. Distance, distance, sand and sky. Space, nothing but space. A vacant world, an empty heaven.

Billowy waves of sand reach away to remote horizons. A half-buried temple stares out from its uncovered tomb, stares through the glare and the heat and the silence. There's a mirage, or as Arabs call it "The Pool of Angels" at which neither man nor beast may slake his thirst.

In places a ribbon of fertile shore divides the river from the waste, an arable strip so narrow that a date palm at the water's edge will cast its shadow into the desert.

Ten miles above the mouth of the Atbara River, Zeidab Plantation occupies the west bank of the Nile, a patch of silt deposit that wedges itself between the nourishing waters and the desert. Jaalin Arabs have cultivated this strip for so many centuries that tradition fails to keep a record. The

Jaalin had *shadoofs* and *sakiehs* lifting water to feed their hungry crops, while naked men chanted as they toiled, intoning the same sad old water chant that ripples forever along the Nile.

It happened once that some enterprising American glanced at Zeidab and backed his judgment that these level lands were excellent for cotton. He acquired thousands of acres, imported carloads of American machinery and squads of southern negroes. He also imported the idea of creating an Utopian farming community in Africa, incidentally solving the negro problem at home. But Utopia never steamed from the start. Colored gentlemen from America tangled up too promiscuously with Jaalin ladies, and mysterious accidents occurred. So many of his negro Romeos met with fatalities, and Jaalins refused so stubbornly to cultivate with American machinery, that the scheme blew up.

Afterwards a practical Scotch syndicate took hold, one of those hard-headed, red-ink corporations that have no souls. Their chartered purpose was to raise cotton, and McGillivray, the general manager, a human steam engine, proceeded to tackle his job.

Zeidab is practically level, sloping away from the Nile just about as our alluvial lands slope away from the Mississippi River, ideally for irrigation.

A Sudan cotton field must be level, and scrapers made Zeidab smoother than a tennis court. Otherwise the prodigious flow of water now pumped from the river cannot be ditched and distributed to the roots of every plant.

The Scotchman owned about forty thousand *feddan,* or acres, and as early as 1910 actually had eleven thousand under the plow.

Jaalin tenants and croppers still remained skittish about devices of the devil with wheels and clicking sprockets that tore up the soil and smoothed it again at one operation. Allah created no such abomination and they'd have none of it. They stuck to the bull and long wooden beam for a plow. Numbers of them, however, have been induced to abandon their laborious method of lifting water by hand, and buy it from the company's canal at $12.50 per *feddan* per year. In other words, the Sudan tenant pays for water alone nearly twice as much as a tenant in our Mississippi Delta pays for land, cabin, fire wood, pasturage, everything that goes with the soil. Yet the delta negro is always broke while the Jaalin keeps a fat balance in bank.

The Sudan government encourages cotton planting by a low tax on cotton land, together with an advance to farmers as a loan or subsidy. Producers appear before officers at intervals with their tall dignified sheiks to identify them and vouch for the condition of their crops, so that each farmer receives a certain amount of money. The Sudan government also makes advances in the shape of a loan or subsidy, which was done twenty-five years before we Americans invented our Farm Board.

Wage hands and most of the tenants live like Egyptian *fellaheen* in villages of mud and dung huts. More prosperous tenants may have separate adobes for each wife, his group of huts surrounded by a sun-cracked yellow wall, with palm trees for shade and dates.

Irrigation ditches are a constant source of trouble and expense. A few minutes of sandstorm will obliterate those at the desert's edge, and a hundred naked laborers must hurry to open them again.

Along the Atbara River, where American cotton flourishes better than Egyptian, about eighteen waterings are required to mature a crop, but here at the Nile the fields are given thirty drinks each season.

Where it becomes necessary to help a tenant finance his crop, Zeidab does not furnish gingersnaps and sardines, but once every two weeks advances cash proportioned to the amount of land that a tenant cultivates—the same system now being used in Mississippi on Panther Burn plantation.

The average cash rent is about double that paid in our Yazoo-Mississippi Delta, but the value of their product is almost double. Heretofore we have been speaking of plantations 950 miles by river below the junction of the White and Blue Niles at Khartum. From Khartum to Cairo very little land is cultivable, a mere strip at the water's edge of no consequence in world production.

South of Khartum, nearer the Equator, are those

vast unmeasured spaces of the Gezira, between two great rivers.

The Gezira lies perfectly for irrigation from both rivers, and canal waters might be turned upon its millions of rich acres, but the Blue Nile cannot supply enough moisture for Egypt and the ravenous Sudan. For every *feddan* that's wetted in the Sudan, a *feddan* in Egypt might have to go dry. A possible shortage of water, perhaps, was part of England's anxiety when Italy took over the sources of the Blue Nile.

The extent of the Sudan is difficult to estimate, somewhat short of a million square miles, or nearly one-third that of continental United States. Enthusiasts contend that much of its soil only requires water and industrious labor to make the best cotton. Maybe so. Hell only requires air-conditioning and cold beer to make a summer resort. Between Khartum and Wady Halfa land that can apparently be cultivated is confined to the river's edge, so very narrow that a boy might throw a brick across it. For miles there is no strip at all; nothing but desert.

If the country is ever to be developed it will not be done by Jaalin, Berberine, Sudani, Dongalowi, Shillooks or Dinkas. Natives have had their chance for uncounted centuries and never carried a languid attempt at cultivation farther from the Nile than a woman could tote a jar of water on her head. Planting of the Sudan to cotton must be the white man's burden. Whether this may succeed in the future a casual traveler is unable to guess. Yet certain obstacles, seemingly prohibitive, stand out like sign boards. To begin with, the Sudan is not a white man's country. Still less is it a white woman's country, for it is said that white children born there never reach maturity.

White men who try to live in the Sudan all the year around lose their vigor and must seek another climate to pass off its deadly enervation.

It requires a white man's vim and robust determination, as well as time, to conquer the Sudan, and Time is the one element which the white man cannot give, because his power to work disappears with a protracted residence. British army regulations recognize this fact and order their officers to take leave each year, a vacation which must be spent outside of Africa.

Anglo-Saxons may temporarily exploit the land, may send successive streams of energy to be destroyed by the desert, but no country can become the permanent home of our race where they have no wives, no children, and where their usefulness is gone at the end of two or three seasons.

Not long ago somebody gave out the yarn in Mississippi that the Sudan could produce unlimited cotton at two cents a pound. If any farmer got scared let him read a report from the Sudan High Commissioner:

Speaking of their chief cotton enterprise, he regrets that low yields and diseases "have begun to cast doubt on the ability of the Gezira to produce a crop which can be sold profitably at any but prices much higher than those which we are entitled to expect. We shall have to regard the Gezira scheme as on the whole a liability to be liquidated by annual subsidies."

The estimated cost of cotton grown in that region for the past season was forty dollars an acre, and the yield about a hundred pounds. That's forty cents a pound, instead of two cents.

3

Until the past year or so southern farmers never wasted a thought on Brazilian rivalry, and statisticians didn't mention it as an important cotton producer like the United States, India or Egypt. Now, and suddenly, we hear that country acclaimed as the "coming empire of cotton," sure to conquer world markets and throw our cotton belt on relief. Other observers, however, refuse to get panicky.

In the spring of 1936 Colonel J. E. Edmonds, well-known economist of New Orleans, sailed for South America to investigate recent activities, and published three articles in *The Saturday Evening Post* for August 10th, August 31st and September 7th, 1935. To his opening story he gave the significant title:

MUCH OBLIGED

Bows Brazil to Uncle Sam's A.A.A.

"Much obliged" stresses the contention that crop reduction in the United States has encouraged foreign competitors to raise cheaper cotton.

Colonel Edmonds was born on a Mississippi plantation and felt anxious about the vast areas of virgin soil that might put his planter friends out of business. So he travelled all over South America viewing cotton, from afoot, horseback, from motor cars, railroads, boats, and airplanes. At night in hotels he talked with experienced growers and traders from Texas, from Bremen, Liverpool, Mississippi, Osaka, men whose money and energy were bringing gin machinery to Brazil, and cotton oil presses. He saw big operators planning if not actually building highways, railroads and steamship docks to transport the harvest from rapidly expanding fields.

Their systematic procedure alarmed the New Orleans economist who says, "A movement is here getting under way that may be comparable only with a movement of the same sort which began in the United States in 1800 and did not end until 1933— the march of cotton from the Atlantic Seaboard to southern California. The same movement in the past has served to awaken drowsing people, to shift population masses, to open new trade routes, to set nations on new pathways, and make history.

"Much Brazilian cultivation is slovenly, but the

country could show thousands of clean cotton acres, heavily fruited and ready for the picker."

The State of São Paulo alone, as its officials assured Colonel Edmonds, can produce about two million bales with its present labor supply. Since 1933 Brazilian exporters have been collecting world prices as influenced by the American cotton policy.

"South Brazilians are willing to grow more cotton as long as they can get $28.00 a bale for lint, seed and all; equivalent to North American growers realizing a shade above 5¢ a pound for lint, with a comparative rate for seed.

"The Northern zone has just harvested nearly seven hundred thousand U. S. bales with the promise of a million for 1935-6. The whole republic is much larger than our continental United States, the one great country on earth which possesses a tremendous space of good soil and a pleasing climate still not turned to use. Observers from Egypt pronounce its river valleys just as fertile as that of the Nile, and as adaptable to cotton.

"During the Civil War in America, Dom Pedro II prodded his people into a quick shift to cotton, yet they soon went back to coffee because cotton was too much trouble.

"During 1920, when weevil ravages seemed to have doomed our Southern Belt, Europe again sent delegations to see if Brazil's production could not be stimulated, but the crop was barely sufficient for coarser textile needs at home, and cultivation was in the hands of the least capable and least industrious.

"The native mind stuck to coffee and everybody went broke until the United States initiated its reduction program so that under plowing up and restrictions American prices rose and Brazilians saw that they could grow cotton and sell it for less. Foreign experts are now swarming here, and yields have increased to such an extent that cotton which in 1933 ranked ninth on their list of exports, had in 1934 taken second place, next to coffee.

"Their cotton is completely substitutable for United States standard grades and staple which can be marketed at figures that will bankrupt every cotton farmer north of the Gulf of Mexico.

"Exports during 1931 amounted to only 51,000 bales, which during ten months in 1934 had risen to 406,000 bales. In June 1935, official estimates placed the current output at 1,770,000 bales. If present ratios of increase be maintained, the crop available here for export by 1940 should be 38,000,-000 bales."

Many Americans of wide experience in Brazil agree, at least partially, with Colonel Edmonds, notably such operators as Mr. W. L. Clayton and Mr. John H. McFadden, Jr., former president of the New York Cotton Exchange, who believes that these new fields "give every indication of out-stripping all others as a formidable competitor.—Half a million bales produced in São Paulo were sold to Liverpool and the Continent infinitely cheaper than American cotton, yet at a handsome profit."

"Their great stumbling block," says Mr. McFadden, "is lack of labor." Unlike most countries today there is no unemployment in Brazil. Immigration laws are strict, and a delegation from Japan is now negotiating a proposal under which Japan will import a million bales of cotton in return for Brazil's enlarging her quota on Japanese immigrants.

Officials are apparently taking action, for President Vargas has recommended letting down the bars and remarked, "São Paulo alone will need forty thousand Japanese laborers this year."

ACCO Press, a magazine published by the Anderson-Clayton Company of Houston, Texas, says, "Brazil alone—disregarding India, Egypt, China, Argentine, Peru, Mexico and Russia—Brazil alone has millions of acres of cotton land the potential production of which is more cotton than would be required to supply the markets of the world. The people are now alert to advantages offered by our artificial price structure, and are bending every effort to establish themselves in foreign markets which our national policy is handing to them on a silver platter."

Brazil's enthusiastic Minister of Agriculture announces, "We are entering the Golden Age of Cotton."

In spite of Brazil's rosy picture certain alphabetic officials at Washington, D. C., remain unterrified, and one of them is quoted as commenting: "The expansion in Brazil has been seized upon and magnified by interests in this country to stampede American cotton growers into abandoning a program which has lifted them out of a four-year depression."

Honorable Daniel C. Roper, U. S. Secretary of Commerce, insists that Brazil's greater yield was due to highly beneficial weather conditions, growing a crop of 960,000 bales in 1933, and for next season estimated at one and a quarter million bales. "But," continues Mr. Roper, "if climatic conditions should revert to normal, their production will drop materially, rather than increase."

Star-gazers predicted upwards of a million bale crop, and believed it so financially that Brazilian speculators plunged on the future board at Liverpool. Plunged and got stung, badly stung, for their million bale dream ginned out a reality of 350,000, and losers hustled mightily to settle their debts.

Department heads at Washington deny that our cotton program has been greatly significant in foreign production, while other skeptical people ask questions:

"Brazil led world production from 1781 to 1800 when our southern states took and held first place until our ports were blockaded during the Civil

War. At that period of cotton famine Dom Pedro tried to stimulate permanent production, yet his people failed to respond even when the bait of a dollar per pound dangled before their eyes. Such extravagant prices were offered that in 1872 Brazil shipped 700,000 bales to England, then practically abandoned cotton because it was too much trouble. Why did their exports drop to 51,000 bales in 1931? If Brazil wouldn't take the trouble from 1862 to 1868 at more than a dollar per pound, why should they go mad in 1936 over 12-cent cotton? Soil and climate are the same, and there has been no revolutionary change in the energy of their agricultural population."

Mr. Cully Cobb of Georgia, chief of the Cotton Section A.A.A., says, "No, sir, we are safe. So long as we don't boost the price above 15 cents nobody can take our foreign markets away from us."

At this point the Bankhead brothers chime in, "Other countries have tried it. It can't be done."

Nevertheless our annual exports have undoubtedly declined by three and a half million bales—another fact to consider.

Mr. Oscar Johnston of Scott, Mississippi, knows cotton at least as well and possibly from more different angles than any man alive. He is a successful cotton lawyer, cotton banker, Assistant Secretary of the Treasury in charge of the cotton pool, and a dirt farmer who studies cotton culture. After digesting all the facts Mr. Johnston concludes, "The general feeling is that Brazil does not constitute a serious threat to American cotton. . . . Some big operators think differently."

There we are again. Take your choice of hostile viewpoints which this volume makes no attempt to reconcile.

4

Three ruinous years of weevil ravages in 1921, 1922 and 1923, cut our Southern crop in half, and foreign growers felt cocksure that by 1932 the United States would not be able to mature a single bale of cotton.

White folks got excited and Cunnel Rye orated mightily at the Court House, which didn't worry Wash Johnson, for Wash never bothered his head about the pest. Sufficient unto the day is the weevil thereof.

The *Country Gentleman* at Philadelphia became disturbed over the South's impending ruin and sent an experienced staff writer, Professor E. V. Wilcox, to learn the worst. In the course of a globe-circling investigation, Professor Wilcox visited every continent and plenty of islands, then published his reactions in the *Country Gentleman* for February 1932 and July 1933.

His observations were made a little upward of four years ago, and however accurate at the time must now be reconsidered in the light of world changes that have since occurred. By permission we quote some of his more important statements:

"The British Cotton Growing Association for over thirty years has promoted cotton planting everywhere except in the United States, hoping to get raw material without buying it from us. France, Belgium, Portugal and Italy were induced to embark on a similar program.

"The American crop in 1931 exceeded 16,900,000 bales, more than 60% of the world's supply, while outside of India where cotton has been grown four thousand years, the British Empire had worked up to only 300,000 bales.

"French officials concluded that by spending $75,-000,000.00, their African colonies might yield as much as Belgium produced in the Congo—that is to say somewhere around 40,000 bales.

"We hear about scores of new cotton regions, each of which may expand into a veritable Cotton Empire, yet none of them have as yet materialized.

"During the 1932 season, the United States, India and Egypt produced 80% of the world supply. In the two Americas, North and South, our Northern share was 90%. Nine tenths of the cotton produced in 1932 by the British Commonwealth of Nations came from Mother India.

"It is easy to see why Russia has fallen so far short of her five year plan quota. The new Russian cotton regions lie in about the same latitude as Boston, St. Paul and Seattle."

"In 1932 in all these new regions," quoting now from Mr. A. P. Demidov, "there was a harvested area of 261,000 acres and a crop of 10,300 bales, or about twenty pounds per acre of very low cotton with undeveloped fiber, representing from 10% to 50% of the total receipts.

"Russian cotton yields per acre are steadily declining and are now only 45% of the 1915 crop.

"Taking into consideration," Mr. Demidov continues, "that all irrigated land available for cotton is used at the present time, it is evident that Soviet production has reached its limit for many years to come."

"Aside from Egypt," says Professor Wilcox, "no part of the Continent of Africa has qualified as a first class cotton country." He cites failures in Algeria, Uganda, Nyasaland, and down the line to Southern Rhodesia.

"A British cotton expert after visiting Nigeria and the Gold Coast, reports, 'Long-continued efforts to promote cotton growing have been unsuccessful on account of very low yield. Natives will not grow cotton for the reason that food crops are more profitable.' "

Professor Wilcox goes on through the catalogue of other fields, then sums up the natural advantages of our own Cotton Belt:

"For four thousand years, or longer, according to Chinese tradition, the world has busied itself in

searching out the best localities to grow cotton. . . .
Notwithstanding its diligence, only about 82,000,000
acres have been found, and 45,000,000 of these are
in the United States.

"We have a better climate, better land, a more intelligent population that understands cotton and
loves its culture. Our whole army of growers,
renters and laborers are superior to those of any
other cotton country. . . . "In the past few years I
have visited over forty of the chief cotton-growing
regions of the world, and have yet to find a place outside the United States where planters get excited
about cotton so long as the market price is under 20¢.

"Throughout East Africa, in Central and South
America, growers tell me they see little profit in
cotton below 20¢, yet 15¢ cotton for five years would
make our South the most prosperous farming section on earth."

Other intelligent observers estimate the possibili-
ties of Egypt where some eight million *feddan* may
be successfully cultivated. Remember, however,
that Egypt is more densely populated than any
country of Europe, and first of all the soil must
feed its people. Better cultural methods and seed
selection might increase the yield, but in acreage
they have about played the limit. We have actually
seen Egyptian crops expand from one and a third
million in 1931 to a million and three quarters in
1934.

Mother India is in much the same position, or rather worse off where it comes to diverting land from food stuff. Agricultural missionaries from America are teaching the natives to grow bigger crops on the same amount of land, besides improving their staple. India knows what it means to go hungry, to see gaunt figures squatted at the roadside, so the people resent and protest against any reduction of food areas. Famine, famine is always before their eyes, and 80 per cent of her acres are now planted in things to eat. The United States has none of these troubles; not a stalk of cotton grows on land that's needed for any other crop.

After a recent tour of the South, Professor Wilcox says: "I came back prepared to bet on our cotton planters against the whole world. There's no spot on earth better suited to cotton than the American Cotton Belt. No people better qualified than our own cotton planters, and no competitior can produce the staple at so low a cost."

Southerners might prefer to believe this, rather than contrary reports. Yet we mustn't stick our heads in the sand like an ostrich, for the ostrich lays herself liable to a rear-end collision.

XXIV

TOO MUCH COTTON

WASH JOHNSON'S mule leaned against the fence and laughed. Even to a mule it seemed comical that his trifling master had over-exerted himself and picked too much cotton.

At the end of that bountiful season, 1931, every grower in the Belt had done the same thing, produced too much staple. One-horse farmers jammed the roads with wagons of seed cotton. Planters trucked tons upon tons from fields that like the pitcher of Baucis seemed never to go dry. Two million growers delivered raw fibre to thousands of gins that kept running day and night. Seed rattled in their hoppers, and foamy lint flowed into presses. Bales, bales, bales were rolled on to gin platforms. Bales, bales, bales were stacked in pasture lots. Bales, bales, bales in freight cars stagnated on side tracks. Trucks roared away to Memphis, Vicksburg, Galveston. Barges floated down the Mississippi River laden with cotton, more cotton, more cotton for New Orleans. Warehouses were stuffed full, tier upon tier, brimming over. Ports became congested, inland towns crowded, and plantations packed with what is called the "world's visible supply." Visible? Sure it's visible. You can't hide a bale of cotton, and ginners reported the turning out of eighteen million bales. Visible supply! Traders knew exactly where to put a finger on every one of them; so many thousand stored in warehouses at Houston, so many other thousands awaiting shipment from Norfolk, stocks in the mills at Providence, cargoes afloat between New Orleans and Japan—each bale accounted for and representing a dead weight that bore down the price.

Planters had long dreamed of a bumper crop that would pay their debts, while small farmers had visions of lifting the mortgage and buying an automobile. Their dream changed to a nightmare, mountains of cotton that wouldn't buy food or clothes. What could be done with millions of bales that nobody wanted? On July 31st our unspun staple, most of it unsold, reached the staggering total of thirteen million bales which must be "carried over" to next season. A normal "carry over" amounts to about five million bales, sufficient to insure dependable stocks and provide against cotton famine. Thirteen million! Wow!

Spinners nibbled at this gigantic pile with as little effect as if a mouse were nibbling at the Rocky Mountains. Of course the bottom dropped out and cotton fell, fell, fell until by June 1932 it was worth less than five cents at New Orleans, nearly touching the all-time low of four and three-eights cents in January 1845.

Editors got busy ladling out "Advice to Farmers"

which sounded like Horace Greeley's famous admonition, "For your crop of broom corn, be sure to plant the striped handle variety."

It's no marvel that people were dazed. Ten years ago the Cotton Belt faced disaster because they couldn't produce staple against boll weevil attacks. Numbers of them abandoned their farms and hunted for jobs in town, or went on relief. Others bucked up and found a way out by poisoning the pest with ground machines and airplanes. Plowing between the rows kept their crops clean and mulched with hot dust so that larvae died. Sweat and elbow grease conquered the pest. Now, as a reward for ten years' labor and an abundance of cotton, again the growers found themselves confronted by starvation in the midst of plenty.

Our wisest leaders didn't know what to do. Neither did the wheat farmer, the hog raiser, the manufacturer in New England or bankers of New York. But we speak only of cotton, not the universal Slough of Despond in which mankind was floundering.

A bewildered government at Washington fumbled around to help, "fumbled" because nobody had or could have a clear idea of what might pull us out of the hole. Any desperate expedient would be tried. Uncle Sam loaned money to farmers on their cotton, and opponents denounced his "pegging" of prices. Whatever was suggested drew a fire of protest. Then came the "plow-up" program, the destruction of growing crops, and met a barrage of condemnation against such an unprecedented crime.

Yet it is a curious fact that this crime, if we call it a crime, was not without precedent, because colonial officials in Virginia more than three centuries ago actually burned low-grade tobacco and held off the market a considerable part of their crop for the identical reasons that made Wash Johnson plow up his cotton.

Those of us who imagine that cotton growers were up against a brand new trouble might glance backward three hundred and seventeen years to Virginia and Maryland where planters grew tobacco exclusively, produced a huge surplus, lost their foreign markets, then tried to bolster up a ruin by the same props that we are using today.

Three hundred and seventeen years ago an ordinance of James City, Virginia, declared tobacco to be currency, which the treasurer of the colony must receive at a "pegged" price of three shillings per pound, exactly as our Federal Farm Board pegged the price of cotton by a sixteen-cent loan. A year later young English women were imported by Jamestown planters as wives, and paid for at one pound of weed in exchange for one pound of wife, 120 pounds per girl.

Virginia and Maryland became shackled by the single crop system, and under British law could not ship tobacco except to England where King James sold monopolies for personal profit. Royal favorites

laid such heavy exactions on the trade that smokers
were unable to buy and consumption declined. The
same objection is urged today, that artificial price
raising has lost our foreign markets.

During the years from 1620 to 1640, tobacco
values sagged from three shillings per pound to three
pence. Compare that with the cotton slump from
December 1922 to December 1932—almost the same
proportion.

Colonial legislatures attempted then, as we are attempting now, to solve the problem of overproduction by law. They tried to fix the price in terms
of English money; tried to maintain a parity with
other products; tried to limit the per capita production, and burned tobacco that could not be sold.

Farm experts, wearing wigs and knee panties,
preached the gospel of diversification, exactly as
agents of the Agricultural Department pleaded with
cotton addicts to raise more food.

Virginia proposed a compact with Maryland fixing a price below which planters would refuse to
sell. They also suggested a "holiday year" when no
tobacco at all should be planted, and three centuries
later Louisiana enacted this scheme into law.

We find the arguments and complaints of those
times rehashed in newspapers of 1931 to 1936—"foreign competition"—"protest against the tariff"—
"middlemen"—"politics"—"Wall Street."

Virginia and Maryland did not invent their make-
shifts to boost the value of tobacco. Already those

expedients were old, old, old, some of them being used by the Emperor Constantine when a depression paralysed imperial Rome. With Constantine's example before him Diocletian also "pegged" the price at 26 cents per Roman chicken; skilled workmen received 44 cents for a twelve-hour day, the artist $1.32. There's nothing new under the sun, certainly not in wage scales or governmental price-fixing.

During the early eighteen-fifties cotton dropped to seven cents, when farmers assembled in convention to argue again about overproduction and low prices. "The Florida Plan of 1851" was announced, then "The Macon Plan." A huge concourse gathered at New Orleans in 1905 with fiery orators, waved their flags and the bands played "Dixie." Ninety years of conventions and speeches accomplished exactly nothing. "Gentlemen's agreements" to limit acreage always ended in bigger crops, for which again we have a precedent.

An ancient Dutch yarn tells of the burgomaster who rendered such noble services that his people arranged a testimonial, a popular tribute where everybody should chip in. The scheme was to present their beloved official with a gift from the entire community, a vast tun of wine into which each man, woman, and child should pour a single bottle.

It might have been a splendid gesture if one thrifty old Dutchman hadn't conceived the idea of pouring in a bottle of water, that cost nothing, and wouldn't be noticed.

Flags waved, bands played and bunting fluttered at a patriotic celebration when the tun was broached and contained nothing but water, not one solitary drop of wine.

Jeerers claim that "gentlemen's agreements" turn out like that. Every farmer rushes home from the convention and doubles his own production, believing that the others will reduce.

2

Years of effort at voluntary association had failed. Growers couldn't get together except for speeches in the Farmer's Alliance, and by satchel-mouthed demagogues eager to save the dear farmer. As Mark Twain once observed, "Everybody cusses the weather, but nobody *does* a darn thing about it."

Nothing was actually done until the morning of August 29th, 1931, when the legislature of the sovereign State of Louisiana passed House Bill No. 1, a bill that read in part:

"The planting of cotton seed for the purpose of raising cotton is hereby prohibited in the State of Louisiana during the calendar year of 1932. Further, the gathering of cotton grown in said year, and the ginning thereof is prohibited."

An incredible revolution. Virtue had been changed to vice, making it a criminal offense to plant one solitary cottonseed within the fecund soil of Louisiana. If the sun were blotted out, if the Mississippi River should suddenly flow northward, these folk could not have been more utterly stupefied. Thousands of farmers knew nothing but cotton, cotton, cotton. From its crude beginnings one hundred and forty years ago the culture of cotton had gradually driven all else from their fields, except sugar in southern parishes and a little tobacco where that could be profitably grown. The entire population of Saxons, creoles and blacks was born in cotton, bred in cotton, and generations had died in cotton. For a century cotton had been the sole reliance of slaves and freemen. Cotton brought them their only cash. Cotton had fed and clad and educated their children. Cotton had paved their roads, constructed their levees, built their churches and maintained their government. Without cotton the world was a blank, a void and barren desolation. So their universe turned upside down.

Cotton farmers in the legislature passed this bill, men who plowed and hoed and picked with their own hands; yet it seemed grotesquely impossible for them to comprehend that if any person now dared to plant a seed of cotton, state police would destroy it.

Numbers of people outside of Louisiana asserted that Huey P. Long, Governor, United States Senator, dictator and despot, all rolled into one package, had crammed his pet notion down the throats of a helpless legislature. This was utterly untrue. Among the personal friends of this writer were members of both Houses, gentlemen whose inde-

pendence can never be questioned. Many of them
had always fought Governor Long. It was the same
Senate that barely failed by two-thirds vote to ac-
complish his impeachment. These men speak out
fearlessly, yet every one of them voted for House
Bill No. 1 *because their farmer constituency demanded it.*

One member of the Lower House, a planter of
ability, said: "I have four thousand acres of cotton
land, and heretofore could borrow forty or fifty
thousand dollars whenever I needed it for a crop.
Now it's impossible for me to raise a thin dime on
that property.—It is already a *fact* that we cannot
produce five-cent cotton. Why not make it the *law*
and reap some benefit?"

Two generations ago everything else was cheap
and the South might struggle along for a while on
low-priced staple; but a planter's overhead expenses
—taxes, freight, supplies—have so doubled and re-
doubled that to market a pound of cotton at five
cents would cost twice as much as he gets for it.
Where a farmer is flat broke, no cash, no credit, he
cannot blindly persist in ginning lint if he must
pay a loss of five cents a pound just for the fun of
wrestling with a hoe and pulling the bell-cord over
a mule. It simply cannot be done.

Louisiana realized that she alone could not accom-
plish such a project, for that state gins only 800,000
bales. The cooperation of Texas with 5,000,000
bales must be secured; a million and one half in

Arkansas; Mississippi's million and a half. Unless the cotton-growing states joined hands almost unanimously in a common cause, Louisiana's balloon blows up.

To cover this contingency House Bill No. 1 provided that Governor Long should suspend its action by proclamation issued on or before January 15th, 1932, if by that date the states producing three-fourths of our staple had not similarly prohibited its planting. By setting the proclamation date at January 15th, ample time was allowed for Louisiana to plant cotton if the expected reinforcement declined to follow suit.

First the bill was sent to Texas, for whatever be done Texas must blaze the trail. After a red-hot discussion Lone Star legislators refused to swallow the pill of total prohibition. Instead they passed a law by which production was cut down fifty per cent, with certain regulations for rotating crops.

A special session in Mississippi adopted the Texas statute. South Carolina wanted to go farther, and Arkansas might have fallen into line, perhaps Alabama; while the whole South stewed in a ferment of disputation, and patriotic men expressed conflicting views. A Georgia ginner found this note posted on his door:

We, the farmers of Jenkins County, ask you to close down this gin at once. We pray God you will cooperate and help us save women and children from hunger and cold until something is done to lift the present depression. We are in favor of Gov. Long's proposition. Be governed accordingly.

For fear of a mob the gin stopped work. Perhaps this incident was only an isolated flare-up, or it might have shown how the wind blew in Georgia. Yet as a state, Georgia did nothing.

Senator J. N. Bailey of North Carolina, in a speech at Raleigh, sounded his solemn warning against all attempts at governmental control of production in America as bolshevistic and communistic, "proceeding along the road to Moscow and to Rome."

Never before in the pathfinding progress of this republic had any legislative body taken such drastic action as that of Louisiana, and behind it lay the tragedy of desperate people. Starvation stared them in the face. They had plenty of cloth stuffs to sell the world, but women couldn't buy dresses and men couldn't buy pants. A ghastly jest! Hordes of ragged farmers throughout the Cotton Belt had piled up such an abundance of potential garments that they themselves hadn't a legal covering to hide their nakedness. Modest families shrank out of sight; shame kept them away from church; over-exposed children could not go to school, and tattered neighbor no longer visited tattered neighbor. Not all of these were negroes who by jungle heredity might slosh along in birthday clothes. Thousands were white men, white girls, white boys, self-respecting Americans.

The "No cotton law" that contemplated such a breaking of ancient idols could not be passed without stirring up a storm of protest, and many objections were not to be laughed off. The City of New Orleans dreaded with good reason that having no cotton to handle in 1932 would add to an unemployment crisis which was already acute. Great compresses must lie idle; classers, samplers, brokers and clerks be thrown out of jobs, with hundreds of stevedores and dock laborers who load the bales on ships.

These contingencies were hotly discussed, but as usual nothing happened. Other states declined to declare a "holiday," the Louisiana bubble burst, and left our cotton belt dangling in thin air.

XXV

WHY WASH JOHNSON PLOWED UP HIS COTTON

THE first legislative shot fired by Louisiana proved itself a dud. Sister states declined to join a "cotton holiday" as colonial planters three centuries ago had refused to declare a "tobacco holiday." Governor Long suspended the ineffective law, and growers began preparing for their crop of 1932.

The farmers had no plan, they never have. They are supposed to be intelligent agriculturists, yet had learned nothing at the University of Hard Knocks. The most ignorant tenant who ever hopped clods along a furrow had been warned time and time again that thirteen million unsold bales were already tiered up in warehouses, scarcely worth picking and ginning. Nevertheless, every fellow for himself and devil take the hindmost, they tightened their galluses and set to work breaking up greater areas of land to produce a bigger crop in 1932.

All around them solid financial institutions were shaking. National banks that had been regarded as Gibraltars of strength popped like a pack of firecrackers, and swept away the savings of citizens who went to stand in bread lines.

Farmers didn't hear this noise, or refused to listen,

refused to think. In a sort of stupor they stumbled across their fields, urging the mule and guiding the plow, resolved to work harder and grow two bales instead of one. One bale at five cents would bring twenty-five dollars, so to get fifty dollars they must sell two bales. None of them seemed to consider that with a double crop their cotton could not be sold at any price.

Anyhow, whether they thought or not, two million farmers plowed and planted and chopped for one of the biggest crops that had ever flourished in the Belt. Operations of that year piled up more cotton, more cotton on top of what was already stored in warehouses, adding two million unneeded bales to the surplus of the world. So at the close of 1932 we "carried over" an excess above fifteen million bales. Spinners made no bids for it because they could sit still and smile at enough fibre to keep the world's spindles whirring for a full year. Even if no other seed were planted in 1933 the visible supply already equalled twelve months' consumption.

For several seasons the Belt had grown good crops, and two whoppers followed at exactly the wrong time when mankind was wearing old breeches because they had no money to buy new ones. Added to this was the nationalistic "Buy at Home" crusade in various countries that formerly bought from us. "Buy at Home" is a patriotic slogan, but there's a joker in it, for if Americans bought only at home we

10,000,000 ACRES OF GROWING COTTON WERE PLOWED UNDER

must sell only at home, and domestic markets cannot consume what we produce.

Foreign demand for cotton fell off under the weight of this heavy carry-over, and prices sank below the six-cent level; sank everywhere. Egypt felt the same pinch, so did the half-fed millions of India; Brazil, Peru, and cotton growers throughout the world were utterly impoverished. Big National banks continued to fail, more than a thousand of them in 1931-32. No trust company or other institution seemed to be safe, especially those that had loaned money on farm securities and could not collect a dollar.

Wheels of industry stopped and millions of American workmen were thrown out of employment. Nobody went ahead except the farmer and politicians, for that was a campaign year when President Hoover was re-nominated by the Republicans, with F.D.R. as the Democratic standard bearer.

It does not sound like an act of sanity, yet next spring cotton farmers bulged on again, stubbornly, blindly, to stack up greater masses of fibre in 1933.

The season opened ideally for germination of seed. Stalks grew rank and blossomed like a flower garden until blind men could see that, barring some climatic disaster, our Belt would produce another eighteen million bales. Absolute ruin confronted the South when President Roosevelt was inaugurated March 4th, 1933, and immediately proceeded to do something about it. Right or wrong, legal or illegal, things were done.

By Act of May 12th, 1933, Congress set up a gigantic organization known as the Agricultural Adjustment Administration to deal with all farm commodities, including cotton.

Cotton was by far our strongest magnet for attracting other people's money, and presented the greatest urgency, because unless prompt action were taken to prevent it, millions of new unneeded bales would be dumped upon our surplus.

The wrangle has now become ancient history so we pass over constitutional objections and economic objections to tell what was actually done against a storm of protest. Authorities at Washington made a classification of cotton lands based upon their average yield for the past five years, and planned to destroy crops then growing on ten million acres. For lands so taken out of production, farmers were paid a ratable rent per acre, which included a fair allowance for money already expended. Funds to pay the farmers were raised by a "processing tax" on manufactured cotton, a tax which the Supreme Court of the United States afterwards declared invalid.

Growers throughout the Cotton Belt held mass meetings and organized local volunteers to cooperate with Uncle Sam. Committeemen in every voting precinct knew how much cotton their neighbors had been producing and saw that allotments were equitably made.

When this project was first suggested, conscientious objectors predicted that farmers would go wading in the public trough and place their yields at fancy figures so as to extract more cash from the government. Some few did show a disposition to grab, but popular sentiment was against them. A splendid sense of service developed in every county where volunteers without pay saw that the plan was honestly administered.

Croakers also made the prophecy that millions would be squandered on lands that were never plowed up. That didn't happen; no petty grafter could get away with it. Unless he destroyed his own cotton, a resolute community ran the plows for him.

On the most fertile alluvial lands that grew long staple, the government paid as high as $20 an acre. Upland farmers who struggled to scratch a living out of barren hillsides that should have been abandoned long ago, didn't get much pay from Uncle Sam, because their worn-out, gully-washed soil was estimated to yield only a hundred and twenty-five pounds of inferior lint per acre, as against more than a bale of finer grade on rich river bottoms.

Based upon average production, Secretary Wallace fixed a sliding scale of compensation, ranging from seven to twenty dollars, and everybody got a proportionate rate. Many a planter destroyed five hundred acres, and one of them tore up three thousand acres—nearly five square miles. Eighty per cent of the growers signed a voluntary contract under which acreage was reduced 35 per cent.

The meanest man on earth, according to Wash Johnson's notion, is a brute who pulls up young cotton or kicks a widow woman's dog in the creek. That's the Southern idea of low-down depravity, for although Wash is not sentimental, he loves a cotton patch.

His plants were now a little better than knee high, brilliant with red and yellow blooms, their limbs bending under the weight of heavy bolls. Most of the bolls were green, only here and there an early one had turned brown and burst, like an exploded grain of popcorn.

The happy tenant stood gloating over his field when the boss rode up and said, "Wash, get out your mule and plow."

"Yas, suh. What for?"

"To plow up three and three-quarter acres of your cotton."

"Huh?" The negro stared with big round eyes, like two white marbles in a bucket of tar. "Huh?"

"Plow up three and three-quarter acres of this cotton."

"Plow it up? Boss, is you talkin' *sense?*"

The bewildered negro couldn't comprehend, neither did old Beck when Wash obediently brought his mule and stood looking on while a committee of white folks measured off the patch for destruction.

"All right, Wash," the boss pointed, "begin at this
row and plow to here."

"Yas, suh. Yas, suh."

A big gulp choked his throat as Wash set his plow
at the start of the first row.

"Git up, mule," he slapped her savagely with the
lines.

Old Beck had been trained never to step on a
stalk of cotton, and Wash couldn't make her do it
now. He had to wrestle with his plow handles, holding the point sidewise as old Beck followed her path
down the middle.

"Dar now!" At the end of the job Wash wiped
off the sweat and gazed at a swath of wilting plants
that lay upon the ground. "Ain't dat a shame!"

Many good citizens condemn this action as a
crime, yet nobody can deny that our farmers did a
darn good job of teamwork. From the Atlantic Seaboard to the Rio Grande, hundreds of thousands of
them followed their mules across the fields until
ten million acres of growing cotton had been uprooted. By this drastic method of birth control some
four million potential bales were prevented from
coming into existence.

Vast sums of money in small amounts were scattered among the farmers, yet we did not see an orgy
of speeding and spending as had been predicted, for
the simple reason that they rarely got actual cash.
What everybody got was relief from pressure.
Plantation debts were so complicated that a propor-

tion of the tenant's check went to pay the landlord's share of cotton that would have been grown on plowed-up land. Then there was a past-due commissary account. Usually the boss conceded a little cash to Wash Johnson, and mighty little money caused big rejoicing. As a rule the planter endorsed his own check to the bank, or to a merchant for supplies. The whole affair operated as a clearing house to loosen a tightness in the Cotton Belt.

This entire program was voluntary, each farmer deciding for himself whether he would sign up and plow up. On account of curtailment, and because world consumers bought more freely, prices began to rise from 5 cents, 7 cents to 8 cents, 10 cents and above. So after destroying 40 per cent of a fine crop it made those farmers hot in the collar to see non-conforming neighbors rake down profits from increased values. Fifteen per cent of the growers had declined to reduce acreage, and the other 85 per cent howled from every precinct in the South. " 'Tain't fair," they wired to Senators and Congressmen. "We cut down our production, and 'tain't fair for those fellows to get the benefit of it." Farmers who had plowed up raised such a racket that Congress answered their demands by passing the Bankhead Act.

Uncle Sam had first suggested to plow up, but it was the people themselves who forced him to change from a free-will arrangement to legal compulsion. Growers who reduced acreage and made sacrifices were determined to prevent an obstructionist from doubling his crop. Unless this were done many of them who had signed up for the previous season proclaimed their intention to kick out of the traces and plant as much cotton as they pleased. There was no law to stop them.

The new statute was a frank attempt at production control; not by reaching into the field but by taxing an excess at the gin where every lock of cotton must go before it becomes a merchantable bale. Each gin in the Cotton Belt became a sort of Customs House, not primarily for collection of duties, but to minimize what we may regard as contraband. The ginner was a bonded officer of the government, and when a grower drove up with a wagon load of seed cotton, the ginner asked to see his exemption certificates. Thereupon the farmer showed a book of coupons, with perforated slips, similar to mileage books formerly issued by railroads. This book represented the pounds of cotton that the grower was permitted to gin, tax free. When the bale rolled out from his press, the ginner weighed it, and tore coupons from the farmer's book for exactly that many pounds, say, 487. After which he attached a tax-free tag.

Should the growers' certificates become exhausted, and he insisted upon ginning more than his allotted quota, he must pay about thirty dollars a bale on the excess. Or, failing to pay, the ginner attached a red tag of warning, a notice to dealers that the government had a lien on that bale which must not be sold until the lien was discharged.

The Bankhead Act was never intended as a revenue measure, and only a small amount of money was collected under it. The law aimed to restrict production of cotton below its annual consumption, so that mills of the world might have time to spin our surplus. In part this object was accomplished. During that season, 1934, some four million bales were kept off the market, the carry-over materially reduced, and values advanced.

2

The Cotton Pool seemed so vast and terrifying to traders that they dreaded it as a Cotton Ocean rather than a pool, for any kind of hurricane might blow up and wreck their business.

The pool was not deliberately planned, but descended like a bequest from the previous administration, and New Dealers paid the inheritance tax.

This transaction has been so thoroughly cussed and discussed that we merely state a few outstanding facts. Under President Hoover's Administration, the Federal Farm Board attempted to stabilize prices, and for that purpose loaned money to farmers on their cotton at 16 cents per pound. This seemed fairly conservative, staple then being worth 18 cents in the open market. But values declined, the Board incurred huge losses, and when the smoke cleared away, Uncle Sam without the slightest intention found himself neck deep in the cotton business, saddled with two and one-half million bales that he had no use for. These were wished off on the Roosevelt Administration and formed a sort of guarantee stock to be used in connection with the 1933 program.

In 1933 the farmer who plowed up, say, sixteen acres of cotton, or a potential yield of eight bales, was given his choice of compensation. He might accept an all-cash rental on the whole sixteen acres, or receive part cash, and in addition take an option to purchase from the government at six cents per pound as many bales as he had supposedly withheld from production.

More than half a million farmers chose the option plan, hoping that because of a smaller crop prices might advance and they'd make a profit.

To handle and market this prodigious amount of cotton, Mr. Oscar Johnston of Scott, Mississippi, was put in charge of the pool. At once the amiable Mr. Johnston became a figure of fear. Big operators trembled at his power, too much power as they complained for one man to wield, and apprehended a panic whenever he might offer "pool" cotton for sale.

No such disaster occurred for the pool manager apparently steered his course with extreme sagacity. Beginning in December 1933, he fed his colossal holdings, little by little, into the mills of the world, at propitious moments and almost without being noticed. Gradually the pool was drained and not once did its outflow cause more than a ripple on the market.

The pool is now empty. Uncle Sam's accumulations were sold at an average price slightly above 12 cents, and $67,000,000 of profits on their future contracts have been distributed among farmers. These sums actually reached the producers in cash and helped to eke out many a slender income.

Draining the Cotton Pool cost our government not one single penny, every expense of overhead, carrying charges, all being liquidated from proceeds of sales. The cotton trade now breathes easier, no longer panicky over two and one-half million unsold bales that would break the markets. Big operators and little operators gathered round on July 31st, smiling happily when they saw the government shut up shop and take down its sign,

---

UNCLE SAM, COTTON MERCHANT

XXVI

SUPPORTERS AND OPPONENTS

FREE America breeds free speech and a pious propensity to criticise whoever happens to be misruling from the White House. None of our presidents have been exempt. Kipling's poem *If* was suggested by abuse heaped upon George Washington because he wouldn't declare war against France; and the kindest remark made by enemies within his own party was to call Lincoln "that baboon at the other end of the avenue."

As it should be. A militant minority puts on brakes and keeps the majority from riding rough-shod. They holler when something hurts, so the hit-and-run driver must stop until they get his number.

Mr. Hoover, our most unfortunate president, entered the White House at a crisis when human wisdom could not have given us a prosperous administration. Accumulated disasters drove him out to be succeeded by Mr. Roosevelt, who also fell heir to attacks and criticism. Ours is a government by political parties, where the "outs" flay the "ins," as Democrats lambasted Mr. Hoover, and Republicans now crucify Mr. Roosevelt.

Mr. Roosevelt is the busiest of executives, making

more experiments and spending more money than all
previous presidents put together. No mortal man,
since Adam began cutting teeth, has shouldered such
complicated responsibilities, or been vested with
such power that the opposition shouts "Dictator,"
"Despot!" Several times the Supreme Court has
nullified his powers as being illegally delegated by
Congress, decisions that the "outs" encored with
whoops of glee.

New Dealers under Roosevelt met worse luck
in the way of criticism than Stand-patters under
Hoover, because their attempts to help Wash Johnson and other farmers to get fair prices for agricultural products built up a powerful antagonism. It
is not here suggested that there was anything sinister
or even unpatriotic in this opposition, for all men
have a right to first take care of themselves and protect their own business.

The plow-up program and acreage restriction of
cotton brought financial loss to many commercial en-
terprises. Crop reduction hit thousands of pocket
books that were dependent upon volume rather than
value, and men usually think as their purses think.
Value makes little difference to the ginner whose
profits are derived from the number of bales that
he rolls out from his press. Of course international
merchants can usually make more money when cotton is high because it bears a larger profit, yet it
may be quite possible for them to get rich by trading in fibre at prices on which the farmer starves.

Railroad companies want their trains to run full
loaded. So do owners of ocean vessels, with armies
of longshoremen and stevedores. Crushing mills
clamor for plenty of seed to make oil, and lint quotations may rise or fall without affecting their
income.

Great warehouses were also hurt. During the period of bumper crops, they added new facilities
to take care of surplus cotton at so much per bale.
Enormous spaces were required to store thirteen million bales, and those unneeded sheds are now empty.
They bring no rent, and real estate owners oppose
the New Deal.

Crop reduction, however, is only partially and
slightly to blame for vacant warehouses in the North
East. Most of that came about for the same natural
reasons that caused the fall of Babylon—a change
in trade routes. Cotton's line of travel for the bulk
of exports has definitely, perhaps permanently, abandoned the North Atlantic Seaboard, diverting this
movement to southern mills and ports on the Mexican gulf.

Two recent developments contributed to this inevitable result. Thirty years ago the South had
practically no spinning mills so cotton went to New
England, or passed through Norfolk or New York
on its way to Europe. Most of the crop was then
grown east of the Mississippi River, a preponderance
that has since shifted to Oklahoma and Texas, who

now send their exports abroad through the Gulf of Mexico.

The southeastern milling section has expanded marvelously, its smooth highways widen the radius of trucks that supply their spindles without resort to railroad or ports. This deprives the carriers of a remunerative traffic. Taken together, the gins, oil mills, railroads, steamships, warehousemen, with hordes of employers, make a formidable antagonism, and most of them fought the New Deal Cotton Policy. None of the New Deal activities was allowed to pass unchallenged, especially during a red-hot campaign. Republican spellbinders assailed whatever the President did, right or wrong; right or wrong the "ins" defended him. That's politics.

"Look!" The G.O.P. keynoter pointed a sarcastic finger at this plank in the Democratic platform of 1932:

We condemn the extravagance of the Farm Board, its disastrous action which made the Government a speculator in farm products, and the unsound policy of restricting agricultural products to the demands of domestic markets.

"Listen," the perspiring G.O.P. orator yells and pounds his table. "Hear what those inconsistent Democrats said about our Farm Board under President Hoover. How do they reconcile that plank with their plow-up program, their slaughter of hogs, and wildcat speculation in cotton?"

Let the reader do his own reconciling. This volume is not a preachment for or against any man or any measure. It merely tries to tell in words of one syllable what various Americans thought and did when Wash Johnson's bale got submerged in the universal deluge.

No statesman seemed wise enough to know exactly what should be done about cotton, or wheat, how to help the factory worker or save our banks. We had plenty of room for honest differences, which our Supreme Court demonstrated by sharp divisions.

Clear-thinking judges put opposite constructions upon New Deal statutes, and it is not surprising that laymen also disputed. As an American humorist once remarked, "I can tell just how much money a feller's got in bank by hearing how he talks about the President."

Take the professional man who has worked hard and laid by a competency. He wants, and has a right to find, profitable investments to secure the comfort of his grandchildren. Large slices are clipped off his earnings by income tax, and spent as he contends on boondogglers. He sees public funds being squandered while national debts pile up for his posterity to pay. Thousands of new officials are created, parasites who eat out his substance, and he dreads what must happen twenty years hence. Such men look ahead, far ahead, and this citizen is against the New Deal.

Here's another man, a college graduate who never

had the knack of making money. A methodical clerk, he budgets his income to the penny, depositing each month a fixed percentage, so much for a rainy day, so much to pay for his modest home. Suddenly, in the wreck of a Trust Company, his savings are swept away. He's thrown out of work. Unpaid instalments accumulate on his mortgage. Children cry for food and the cupboard stands empty. The family must eat, and their father cannot look twenty years ahead or consider the permanent welfare of this republic. His needs are *now*. Right *now*. It is understandable why millions of such Americans are grateful for a boondoggling job that other citizens denounce as criminal waste. The harried father thanks whatever gods there be for a Home Owner's Loan Corporation that tides over his debts and gives him a chance. As an intelligent man he may also wonder where this orgy of spending may lead us in the future; but his hand-to-mouth existence of today is so compelling that he supports the New Deal.

We seem to drift away from cotton, but the sale of Wash Johnson's bale involves our entire social and economic structure.

Thinkers discount partizan harangues on both sides of the political game, while temperate statements of businessmen are entitled to respect.

Wherever cotton in quantity is grown or processed, Anderson-Clayton Company of Houston, Texas, have established themselves. They rank among the greatest staple merchants of all time, with branch houses in China, Brazil, Japan, Egypt, Mexico, Germany, England, Peru and other centers. The firm issues a monthly magazine at Houston, the *ACCO Press,* from whose columns we quote these extracts, assuming them to represent the feeling of international traders. Since then Mr. Clayton may have modified his views, anyhow in 1935 he said:

"Texas, more than any other state in the union, depends upon exports, the chief of which is cotton. 90% of her production is sent abroad, and half of her people are directly or indirectly dependent upon exported cotton.

"Texas is a state of vast surpluses, land, wheat, cotton, petroleum, nevertheless a hundred thousand of its farm families are now on relief.

"A most remarkable thing about world cotton is the fact that during the five years of this depression its consumption throughout the world has been substantially higher than the average for ten boom years immediately following the Great War.

"Mankind is still consuming cotton at a rapid rate. It is only in the United States under the influence of a pegged price, a 35% processing tax and 80% increase in textile labor that consumption lags.

"For ten years following the Great War our Southern Cotton Belt furnished 60% of the world's consumption. Before that time our percentage was greater. During the present season we'll furnish

45%, which means that we have lost our market for about three and a half million bales annually.

"Last year [1934] we doubled our automobile business abroad, nearly doubled copper; sold more than twice as much iron and steel, at the same time losing our cotton trade because the rest of the world undersells us. We commenced losing that trade when the Farm Board started its so-called stabilizing operations. Under the A.A.A. program the consumption of American cotton has followed production downward.

"The Southern cotton farmer has for years sold the fruits of his labor in free markets, while buying everything in a protected market. This has produced an economic inequality, both cruel and unjust.

"Under a continued jacking up of our tariff, a pound of cotton buys less and less of manufactured goods, pays less and less of taxes and interest.

"What the farmer needs is relief from unjust burdens of the tariff; instead we have increased the tariff and placed additional loads on his back through N.R.A. and other nationalistic measures.

"Cotton is grown in a comparatively small part of the earth's surface; it is used throughout the whole world. Hence when one thinks of cotton one must think in terms of world trade. Remember that cotton is not an American commodity, it is a world commodity, and 55% of our American crops must normally be marketed abroad.

"If experience teaches anything it is that nature's

method of automatic regulation through price, arrived at by competitive trading in free markets, is the only system which ever works in world commodities like cotton.

"If we continue the present policy of attempting to make the market pay higher prices through planned scarcity, we must face the eventual loss of all our export markets for cotton. We must find some other use for twenty-five million acres of agricultural land, most of it in the southwest, and other means of livelihood for a million and a half southern families.

"The season of 1929-30 was the first time since Civil War days when consumption of foreign-grown cotton throughout the world exceeded that of American cotton. Largely as a result of the Farm Board's interference in cotton markets, the end of the season 1931-32 saw a carry-over of American cotton throughout the world of thirteen and one-quarter million bales—the largest carry-over by far which has even been known.

"From 1929 to 1932 inclusive we had lost markets to foreign-grown cotton of five and a half million bales.

"Added to this we have almost completely lost our export market for cotton goods, during a period when most other commodities show a big increase.

"The loss of foreign markets is traceably directly to the fact that the American Cotton Policy has priced our cotton out of the market.

"A substantial increase in production in foreign cotton has recently taken place at the same time that the A.A.A. program and Bankhead Bill have caused a great decrease in production here.

"Over fifty countries in the world now produce cotton, and records show that the amount of foreign-grown fibre has just about doubled in the last fifteen years. And they will continue to expand their fields as long as the United States continues to artificially set the price of American cotton at a figure above the world price. This means abandonment year by year of a substantial part of our world market until at the end we will have surrendered practically all such foreign outlets, leaving only the American market using about six million bales annually.

"The only sound policy for relief of our agricultural population is a drastic reduction in the tariff, and recognition of the uncollectibility of war debts, so that our surplus may again find a market abroad at compensatory prices."

Mr. John H. McFadden, an international cotton merchant and former president of the New York Exchange, expresses practically the same opinions as Mr. Clayton.

The Honorable Eugene Talmadge is of course in politics, otherwise he would not have been Governor of Georgia.

Evidently a plain-spoken man, Governor Talmadge goes the whole hog in opposition, and makes no bones about saying, "I did not attend the meeting at which President Roosevelt spoke in Atlanta on Nov. 29th, (1935). I did not by word nor smile nor deed wish to appear hypocritical. I did not wish anyone in America to think I had condoned in any manner the policies of the present Administration."

Just as vigorously he attacked the now defunct A.A.A. and Bankhead Bill. On his suggestion the State of Georgia filed suit against the Federal Government to declare unconstitutional the A.A.A. laws and all processing taxes. His grounds were that Georgia grows cotton at some of its institutions and was required to "sign up" under the Bankhead Bill; if Georgia exceeded her allotment, she must pay a tax or penalty. The state proceeded in her own right and got a quick decision because our U. S. Supreme Court held the A.A.A. unconstitutional.

As part of his contention Governor Talmadge insists:

"Large land owners are responsible for overproduction of cotton and its disastrous effects. Yet the government rewards them with hundreds of millions of dollars of farm aid. And it puts a penalty on the small land owner who had always reduced by diversifying.

"Take the government out of business. . . . If the farmer plants corn and wheat and has a surplus to sell, let him take the price in an open competitive market; likewise cotton, tobacco or any other com-

modity. Then let the same farmer have the right to
buy supplies that he may need in an open competitive
market.

"Farmers of Georgia who acted sensibly in reduc-
ing their acreage while the price of cotton fell con-
tinuously from 1927 to 1932, are now penalized by
the Bankhead Act. But farmers who acted unwisely
and refused to reduce acreage during those years
are now set upon a pedestal and receive vast sums
from the United States Government.

"The farmer is tired of signing up. He is tired of
doing his farming on paper at the government's direction. He is ready to go back to dirt farming, and
I predict that he won't lose the opportunity of
doing so.

"My advice to farmers of Georgia and the United
States is to plant cotton according to their own judgment."

Such utterances are to be gravely considered, but
contrast them with what a certain dirt farmer thinks,
a man who successfully cultivates large plantations
and is highly regarded in Mississippi:

"A little more than three years ago under the sane
administration of President Hoover, I saw national
banks crashing around me, 1035 of them. Local institutions failed and people lost their savings. The
best I could do in that season was to sink fifty
thousand dollars that I had sweated for, and didn't
know how to pay. Other farmers were in a worse

fix because they owed more money and creditors took
their property. Thousands of white men, proud of
their independence, went on relief. Planters had no
idea how they could feed their negroes.

"Since then I have seen the banks re-open and
keep open so that we can finance our crops. Cotton
has more than doubled in value. Hopeless farmers
were able to pay out and get back their land.
Numbers of them now have cash in bank to make
this year's crop without borrowing a cent. I'm no
lawyer to argue about the Constitution, but all of us
have seen these things."

O. Henry once wrote a story called "Roads of
Destiny" in which young David set forth with staff
and scrip to seek his fortune. Three leagues from
home he came to a place where the paths forked, and
the boy didn't know where they led. At random he
took the left branch and met adventures; then came
back to the right fork and met other adventures.

Four years ago we Americans stood at the forks
to choose between Mr. Hoover, who beckoned in one
direction, while Mr. Roosevelt pleaded with us to
go another way. In our wisdom, or folly, we went
with Mr. Roosevelt, and here we stand today. Conditions that surround us are not satisfactory to everybody, but where would we have been had we taken
the other path?

We never hear the airy footsteps of things that
almost happen, and our very blunders, if they are

blunders, may have saved us from worse disaster. We still exercise a freedom of choice at the ballot box, and Mr. Roosevelt, the all-powerful, might have been pulled down at the November elections.

Most of the world is not so fortunate. Two of its ancient nations, Italy and Greece, are supposed to be constitutional monarchies governed by law, while in fact each of them bows to a dictator who recognizes no law except his own unbridled will. Centuries ago Greece boasted of a pure democracy; now her bravest editor is forbidden to comment upon any act of the dictator.

Mussolini announces that "eternal peace does not suit the genius of Italy," while Hitler points to the riches of Soviet Russia and hints at what may be the profits of a successful war. France, under a Socialist premier, shudders on the brink of a Communistic revolution. The fiendishness of mass murder is turned loose in Spain, where Fascists attack the Socialistic government. Most of the world is in turmoil while this country remains quiet, struggling with trouble, yet not resorting to violence.

Four years ago when we stood at the forks of the path, unknown millions of women as well as men roamed about the land, desperate and hungry. They jammed the freight trains; with heads down; sullen and hopeless they trudged along the roads, going nowhere. And we needn't kid ourselves into believing that there's no danger in such an army. Famished mobs elsewhere have robbed and burned and murdered. As patriotic Americans our people might have starved to death without mussing up the map; or might have looted the homes of well-to-do citizens who now protest against high taxes.

Jobless ones, however, kept quiet in the faith that something was going to be done about it. Grant that regiments of idle men and women were employed at non-essential tasks. Grant, for instance, that Vicksburg could have rocked along without the new Post Office. Grant that relief money was lavished on chronic beggars who never did a day's work. Grant every objection, yet perhaps those activities staved off bloody riots, or attempts at revolution.

The other path might have been better, or it might have brought us to a rougher camping spot. Who knows.

XXVII

THE KING THAT WALKS ALONE

AFTER four years of coddling, the Government has knocked all props from underneath King Cotton and taken away his crutches. The King now walks alone with no artificial support, while Uncle Sam pockets his losses like a thoroughbred and bows himself out of business by selling every bale in the Cotton Pool. Growers were fairly well able to finance their present crop through private sources, and we now have no big loans at a "pegged" price, which means that values must depend upon how much consumers will pay in wide-open markets.

It is yet too early to see what may be the lasting effects of the A.A.A., the Bankhead Bill, and other New Deal policies that restricted production. Years may elapse before activities in Brazil settle down and show results, either by a deluge of cheap fibre or by slumping back to coffee as Brazilians did after our Civil War when inflated prices fell.

Uncle Sam's help, or meddling, is a thing of the past, and utter ruin as predicted for cotton farmers is still in the future. During the bountiful autumn of 1936, except in drouth-stricken sections of Oklahoma and Texas, growers were so busy gathering a snowy harvest that they had no time to borrow trouble for 1956.

Trade conditions are far more wholesome than they were in 1932 when we confronted a paralysing "carry-over," stacked up unsold and unwanted in warehouses. Consumption has since kept ahead of production and the surplus is reduced to workable proportions, the lightest "carry-over" since 1929-30.

A most encouraging item is the brisk demand by spinners to fill their orders for manufactured goods. Southern mills especially are consuming more and more raw material. As buying power expands, the American housewife must replenish her "linen," which is brevet linen, alias cotton. She hasn't bought a nickel's worth during the depression and sheets are worn out, pillow cases ragged, table napkins full of holes. Shirts and socks and undies to buy, handkerchiefs, curtains, towels—the mills must spin a lot of cotton.

Clothes are coming back in style. Ladies have lowered their skirts from the thigh to the ankle and it is astonishing how much cloth will be required to cover forty million pairs of legs.

Manufacturers formerly insisted that American cotton wasn't fit for first-quality automobile tires which should be made of costlier Egyptian. Experience however has taught them to weave a fabric as durable, or even stronger, from our own staple, so that one factory alone now buys annually five million dollars' worth of delta cotton. This new outlet has grown up, almost leaped up, within recent years. In 1906, Americans drove about one hundred thousand automobiles. Today twenty-seven millions cars go scorching along our roads and burn up cotton, creating a ravenous market that was unknown to old-time planters.

Hunger is the mother of Hustle, so that some of our crop-and-credit farmers are gaining sense enough to grow their own rations. On well-managed properties "live at home" conditions are immeasurably improved. When he plowed up his cotton and the Bankhead Bill restricted his acreage, the farmer found himself with idle land that might be devoted to corn, oats, soy beans, alfalfa and forage crops. He was forced to supply his own table because he couldn't pay for imported grub. The small farmer dug potatoes and coaxed his cabbages to head, while landlords practically starved their tenants into cultivating kitchen gardens. During the worst of the depression negroes lived far better than they had ever lived in boom years. When prosperity returns most of them will forget the lesson, but some of their thrifty habits must stick.

Farmers along the Mississippi River are busy as a switch engine. No storms blew out their open bolls, nor rains beat down their lint into the mud. Grade is exceptionally high, and grade is essential in the delta whose famous long staple commands a premium of two to three cents a pound—ten to fifteen dollars a bale. New Orleans quotations range slightly above 12 cents and with their premiums delta farmers may realize around $70 to $75 per bale. Add $19 for seed and we have a gross return of about $90, as against less than $30 four years ago. Sixty dollars extra on each of eleven million bales runs into real money and will help every human being in the United States.

The fly in the ointment was lack of labor for picking, and farmers want to get their cotton out of the field while it's clean. With so much unemployment around us and relief rolls crowded by able-bodied men supposed to be destitute, it seemed incredible that the planter couldn't get hands to gather his crop. Landlords begged for help and paid $1.25, even $1.50 per hundred pounds. A negro woman at that rate may earn $5 per day, and enjoy herself immensely during the festivities of cotton-picking time.

Some of our relief officials threatened to drop from their rolls every healthy person who refused to work; and those who did pick cotton would be restored to the rolls when they returned. Other officials, higher up, took a somewhat different position and declined to coerce the beneficiaries.

Meantime one need only stand at the Vicksburg Bridge to see great trucks roll across the river loaded with Mexican pickers from Texas. Mississippi planters send hundreds of miles for Mexicans to do a work that it would seem our unemployed home folks should be glad to get. Abundant labor, however, was got together, and the crop was picked out faster than any one before it.

In our Cotton Belt, corn rarely thrives on the same distribution of rainfall and sunshine that grows fine staple. When cotton is prolific, corn usually runs short. This season grain and forage crops are so plentiful that the industrious farmer should produce sufficient food for man and beast. Fields not devoted to staple have yielded generously.

Look at the balance sheet of one small property, 500 open acres and 200 in woodland. The farmer who bought it had made money last year and paid $20,000 cash. After repairing some dilapidated cabins he planted 300 acres to cotton, 200 to corn, soy beans, and hay. The soil is a fertile river bottom, and from the present crop he will gather $24,000 worth of lint, besides the value of his grain and forage. In a single season this little plantation practically returned its cost. That can't be done every year, but one farmer did do it.

The crop of 1936 was somewhat above eleven million bales, not enough to glut the markets. A Government forecast on August 1st indicated upward of twelve millions, but lack of rain on western fields scaled it down. Weather conditions afterward improved somewhat in Georgia and the Carolinas, yet as a whole the crop was smaller than expected.

Mr. Henry Plauche, Secretary of the New Orleans Cotton Exchange, like Mr. Henry G. Hester who preceded him, is known as a "respecter of facts." In his annual report of September 1st, 1936, Mr. Plauche says that general conditions are more favorable, and its most encouraging feature is the retirement of Uncle Sam by closing out his Cotton Pool:

"Last year conditions in the cotton-manufacturing industry were most unsatisfactory. Uncertainties then prevailing, such as the future of the A.A.A., etc., have all been eliminated by judicial decisions.— Passing of these uncertainties has made it possible for the industry to proceed under more normal conditions and with greater confidence."

Operators were also afraid of Congress, and when the Solons went home, as Mr. Plauche naïvely comments, "a material improvement has taken place."

American mills have sold goods freely, making substantial contracts for cloth to be delivered, which assures full operation for many months and pay rolls to workers.

Exports increased more than a million over last season, yet fell short by a million and a half of what was sold abroad in 1933-34.

Japan bought the bulk of foreign shipments, one and a half million bales, somewhat less than the previous season, while Great Britain nearly doubled its takings and so did Germany.

For his 1935 crop the farmer received, counting cotton and seed, $931,000,000 as against $739,000,000 in 1934. Add government benefits and we have a billion dollar total. For cotton alone growers were paid $760,000,000 as compared with $450,000,000 for 1931-32.

Mr. Plauche is not a loose-tongued booster, but confines himself to cold facts, and his report is distinctly encouraging.

Anyhow, King Cotton now walks alone, to stand or fall by his own power in rough-and-tumble competition with fifty other countries.

A FEW BOOKS

This volume is a cotton primer, mostly on the production end. For world-wide market statistics, crops, prices, and other information consult:

Cotton Goes to Market, by Alston Hill Garside, Economist for the New York Cotton Exchange, Frederick A. Stokes Company, New York.

Cotton and the A.A.A., by Henry I. Richards, Brookings Institution, Washington, D. C.

Cotton as a World Power, by James A. B. Scherer, Frederick A. Stokes, New York.

Cotton, by Harry Bates Brown, McGraw-Hill Book Co., New York.

Heritage of Cotton, by M. D. C. Crawford, G. P. Putnam's Sons, New York.

The Story of Cotton, Anderson-Clayton Co., Houston, Texas.

The Inside Story of a Cotton Boll, prepared by National Cotton Seed Products Association, Dallas, Texas.

American Cotton Strangled by American Tariff, by W.

L. Clayton. *Cotton Trade Journal,* International Edition, 1933.

Brazilian Cotton, see International Federation of Master Cotton Spinners and Manufacturers, Manchester, Eng., 1922.

Brazil. Report by Brazilian Government, 1921.

Brazil. Report by P. K. Norris, U. S. Dept. of Agriculture.

Report of Consul-General Carroll Foster, 1935. By J. C. Fornes.

The Tobacco Complex. (Pamphlet) By Dean Henry C. Frey, Louisiana State University, Baton Rouge, Louisiana.

The Marvellous Story of Cotton Seed, by Arthur Coleman in *Holland's Magazine,* Dallas, Texas. Republished *ACCO Press,* August 1935.

Cotton and the Future Contract System, by Munds, Winslow & Potter, 40 Wall St., New York.

"The Senatorial Hearings on Cotton Cooperative Associations held at Memphis, Tenn." October 28th, 1935.

Two volumes of testimony and reports under Senate Resolution 185. And see *Cong. Record,* May 27th, 1936.

"Government Activities in Cotton and Their Effects on the Industry." Address delivered by Mr. Alston H. Garside, Greenville, S. C., April 3rd, 1936.

Cotton and the New Orleans Cotton Exchange. Prof. J. E. Boyle. Country Life Press, Garden City, New York.